Knut Wicksell on Poverty

T0271690

Knut Wicksell is arguably the greatest Swedish social scientist of all time and poverty was a theme that occupied him all his life. Indeed, it was probably this interest that was the main factor in drawing Wicksell away from his studies of mathematics and into economics instead.

Mats Lundahl, a development economist and a specialist on poverty himself, examines Wicksell's thinking in the area and shows that his contribution is a major one.

Mats Lundahl is Professor at the Stockholm School of Economics.

Routledge studies in the history of economics

Knut Wicksell on Poverty

'No place is too exalted for the preaching of these doctrines'

Mats Lundahl

Routledge
Taylor & Francis Group

LONDON AND NEW YORK

First published 2005 by Routledge
2 Park Square, Milton Park, Abingdon, Oxon OX14 4RN

Simultaneously published in the USA and Canada
by Routledge
711 Third Avenue, New York, NY 10017

Routledge is an imprint of the Taylor & Francis Group, an informa business

First issued in paperback 2012

Typeset by Prepress Projects Ltd, Perth, Scotland

British Library Cataloguing in Publication Data
A catalogue record for this book is available from the British Library

Library of Congress Cataloging in Publication Data
Lundahl, Mats, 1946–
  Knut Wicksell on poverty : 'no place is too exalted for the preaching of
these doctrines'/ Mats Lundahl.
    p. cm. -- (Routledge studies in the history of economics)
  Includes bibliographical references and index.

  1. Wicksell, Knut, 1851–1926. 2. Poverty. 3. Population. I. Title. II.
Series.
  HC79.P6L863 2005
  339.4'6--dc22

                                                              2004017247

  ISBN 978-0-415-34427-2 (hbk)
  ISBN 978-0-415-65532-3 (pbk)

To the memory of my teacher Torsten Gårdlund (1911–2003), Wicksell biographer sublime

> I consider no place, not even the pulpit itself, to be too exalted for the preaching of these doctrines.
>
> Knut Wicksell 1880

Contents

Preface

The present book began as an academic accident. I was approached by the Department of Economic History at Lund University to write a chapter for a book on how great economists have looked at the causes of poverty. The suggestion was that I should write a chapter on Knut Wicksell. I was not at all happy with the suggestion and did all I could to turn down the offer. I had read Torsten Gårdlund's masterpiece *The Life of Knut Wicksell* and knew that Wicksell's views were closely linked with those of Malthus, seemingly to the point at which Wicksell at times appeared to be something of a carbon copy, definitely not as original as in his other writings. The department insisted, however, so I gave in and promised to give it a try. I thought I could always write a short account.

At that point I recalled that I had been at a conference outside Lund in 2001, on the occasion of the centennial of the appointment of Knut Wicksell to the chair in Political Economy and Fiscal Law. There, Professor Hitoshi Hashimoto had shown photocopies of the unpublished manuscript that Wicksell had presented to a competition for a scientific prize in France in 1891. Gårdlund had an account of it in his book, and I thought that maybe a study of that manuscript could yield a new thing or two. So I contacted Professor Hashimoto, who kindly sent me the manuscript. Equipped with that and a number of Wicksell's pamphlets that had been in my possession for years, I somewhat reluctantly began to sketch the essay.

In two months I had a manuscript for a small book. It had almost written itself. After having read a few of the central works I saw that Wicksell was arguing in a fashion that looked very much like a general equilibrium system based on the so-called specific factor model. Organizing the book then was easy, I got carried away and the first draft was written in a frenzy.

That draft was circulated to some people with the provisional title *Condoms from the Pulpit*, to make sure that they would read it. However, as Professor Hashimoto gently reminded me, that title was a bit too low for the subject, so in the final instance I changed it, retaining mainly the pulpit.

xvi *Preface*

I am indebted to a number of people, above all to Hitoshi Hashimoto, without whose generosity I would never have seen the *Prix Rossi* essay. Ronald Findlay, Ronald Jones, Bengt Jönsson, Lars Jonung, Christina Rapp Lundahl, Bo Sandelin and Bjørn Thalberg all read the manuscript and suggested a number of improvements. I also benefited from the comments made by two anonymous referees. I hope they are satisfied. If not, the blame is entirely my own. As always, Lilian Öberg has helped me with all kinds of practical details in connection with the preparation of the manuscript. My debt of gratitude to her simply keeps growing.

The book was finished during my stay at the Swedish Collegium for Advanced Study in the Social Sciences (SCASSS) at Uppsala, where the book was also presented in a seminar. I have very much appreciated the congenial and relaxed atmosphere at SCASSS – a veritable water hole in the Swedish academic world.

Mats Lundahl
Uppsala
22 April 2004

Plate 1 Wicksell's cell at Ystad jail.

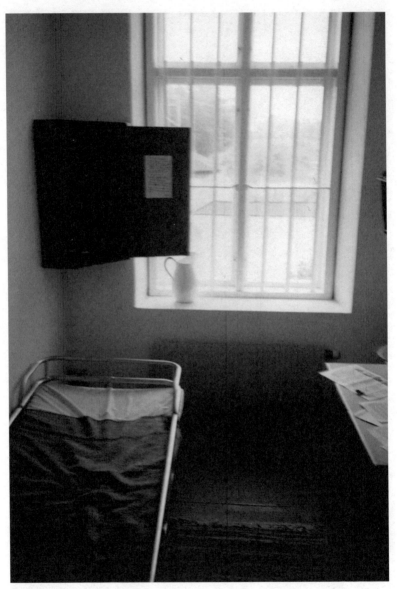

Plate 2 Wicksell's cell at Ystad jail.

1 Introduction

The causes of poverty are a theme that occupied Knut Wicksell for virtually all of his adult life. It was the theme for the speech and the publication that made him a well-known or, rather, notorious public figure in Sweden in 1880, and it was also the theme of two of his last publications: one published in 1925 (Wicksell, 1925), the other, posthumously, just after his death in 1926 (Wicksell, 1926a). It can hardly be doubted that his passion in this matter was one of the factors that made the student of mathematics take an interest in questions related to the social sciences and which pulled Wicksell away from the natural sciences into the study of economics.

The conventional wisdom

Arguably, Knut Wicksell is the greatest Swedish social scientist of all time. However, the subject of poverty and population is one of the few areas in which the conventional wisdom is that he failed to produce anything very original. The only credit usually given to Wicksell for his writings on these subjects is for his views of optimum population. Lionel Robbins (1927: note 118) believes him to be the first to have used the term, but concedes him a mere footnote, whereas Manuel Gottlieb (1945: 291–2) views him as the culmination of a celebrated tradition:

> ... the optimum population concept is one of the culminating points of a large body of tested thought and it was explicitly developed as an analytical tool by some of the path-breaking theorists who established the essential foundations of modern economics: Marshall, Sidgwick, Cannan and – above all – Knut Wicksell. Certainly labeling the theory as a mere rationalization for the cause of population stability or decline or as an 'Anglo-Saxon Theory' is not acceptable.

Joseph Spengler (1983) credits Wicksell with being 'Father of the

Optimum.' J. D. Pitchford (1974: 87) mentions him along with Edwin Cannan and Julius Wolf as 'independently originating the optimum population concept,' and E. P. Hutchinson (1967: 391) calls him an 'early exponent of the optimum population concept.' Monica Fong (1976: 314) argues that 'Wicksell's major contribution to population studies is . . . twofold: (i) the idea of an optimum population size – implicitly a stationary population – and (ii) the idea that this optimum may already have been exceeded.' Mauro Boianovsky (2001: 130) claims that 'the first appearance in print of the notion of "optimum population"' was in Wicksell's *Über Wert, Captal und Rente* (English translation, 1954: 165–6) and that he introduced the concept as such in the first (Swedish) edition of his *Lectures in Political Economy* (Wicksell, 1901: 49).[1]

Exactly how original Wicksell was in his area is open to some doubt, however. In an article written on the occasion of the centennial of the birth of Wicksell in 1951, Erik Lindahl stresses that '*The population problem* was for him primary,' and points out that Wicksell worked with an optimum population concept based on 'where the national product per head attained its maximum' (Lindahl, 1958: 35) but that he did not pursue the concept of optimum population further than this. Joseph Schumpeter (1954: 582), in his monumental survey of the history of economic doctrines, gives Wicksell only limited credit for having 'resuscitated' the optimum population concept.

Wicksell's successor as professor of economics at the University of Lund, Emil Sommarin (1926–7: 29), simply points to his insistence on gaps that remained to be filled:

> Exactly like . . . [Wicksell's] contributions to the population question have assumed scientific importance by demonstrating the lack of knowledge with respect to the regular connections between the elementary factors of the development of population, nativity, mortality and emigration, where a scientific theory is still lacking, he has brought up the necessity of computations of the probable development and distribution across the age groups etc. of the population during the next decades, without which political foresight must be deficient on important points.

The remainder of Wicksell's writings on population is generally considered not to belong to his most original pieces. Thus, writers on Wicksell either tend to pass them by altogether, give them a mere cursory treatment, or state more or less explicitly that they are doctrinaire and lacking in originality. Carl Uhr, in his centennial evaluation of the great Swedish economist, puts the optimum population concept at the heart of Wicksell's demographic writings (Uhr, 1951: 832–4) in his large monograph on Wicksell's contributions to economics; he devotes no more than some scattered remarks on a handful of pages to it (Uhr, 1962: 3, 59–60, 328–9), and in his shorter portrait of Wicksell (Uhr, 1991a) he does not even include it under 'Wicksell's contribution to economics.' Torsten Gårdlund (1996), Wicksell's biographer, uses considerable space to discuss his writings on population but passes no judgment on their quality. Bo Gustafsson (1961: 203), on the other hand, takes a negative stance and refers to his 'uncritical acceptance of the Malthusian doctrine – that with him assumed the character of a socio-political panacea,' what Gustafsson (1961: 226) considers to be one of 'the prejudices of orthodox economic theory.' This is the view that has become the accepted one:

> Wicksell shares with some of his modern counterparts the tendency to relate population to all social problems. According to Wicksell, an end to population pressure would alleviate not only poverty, but also crime, emigration, social inequality, inequality between the sexes, the evils of colonialism, and the need to wage wars, including cold wars . . .

writes Monica Fong (1976: 314), and Rolf Henriksson (1991: 40) refers to Wicksell's 'dogmatism' as soon as it came to the population issue.

As late as 2002, in a full-length text in Swedish on the history of economic doctrines, Lars Pålsson Syll (2002: 241) offered the following summary judgment of Wicksell's writings on the population question:

> Even though in retrospect Wicksell stands out as an extremely homogeneous and for most people sympathetic figure, his dogmatic clinging to the Malthusian ideas colored by Utilitarianism represents an element in his thinking that is difficult to swallow. Developments during the interwar period also rapidly made these ideas become obsolete and made them fall into oblivion. One factor that contributed to this was the comprehensive criticism that the Myrdals subjected Wicksell's population doctrine to. In *Kris i befolkningsfrågan* [*Crisis in the Population Question – sic*] (1934) the doctrine of optimum population is called a 'speculative desk construction', as calculating where this optimum would be appeared impossible. According to the Myrdals, at the root of the very idea was the vision that in the future technological progress would come to an end, whereas the 20th-century reality was different. The imagined scarcity of natural resources was a 19th-century monstrosity. As a matter of fact, technical progress had been so powerful that it 'is on the verge of breaking the institutional framework of our society'.

Strange as it may seem, Wicksell's writings on poverty and population have not been well penetrated by the specialists on economic doctrine. The literature is full of misconceptions of all sorts. Thus, Monica Fong (1976: 311) claims that 'his population writings are few in number.' A look at the reference list of the present work should suffice to prove that the opposite is true (even discounting pieces unpublished until recently).[2] Also, Richard Goodwin (1979: 190), in a contribution presented at a symposium on Wicksell, for reasons that defeat comprehension, managed to get away with the following statement:

> After a scientific training, … [Wicksell] at one point read and got the Malthusian message: perceptively he realized that the issues posed required more serious economic analysis than they had received: accordingly he devoted the rest of his life to that task. Thus he soon came under the influence of the New Economics, marginalism, and felt it superior to Malthus and to classical economics generally. It may well have been this influence *which gradually undermined and ultimately practically eradicated his commitment to neo-Malthusianism.*[3]

Goodwin appears to have been confused by the fact that Wicksell chose to drop the first chapter, on population, from the later editions of his *Lectures on Political Economy*. What he must have been totally ignorant about is that the first chapter appeared as a separate booklet in 1910 and that it was with the second edition of this booklet, written completely in the neo-Malthusian spirit, that Wicksell was busy at the time of his death. 'Although towards the end of his life economics had become his main interest, his old enthusiasm for the population problem never deserted him,' writes Gårdlund (1996: 317). This also refutes Johannes Overbeek (1973: 205), who claims that a speech given by Wicksell in Amsterdam in 1910 'can be considered to be his "last word" on the subject.' Erik Lindahl (1958: 29) has the correct story:

> All through his life he maintained, with remarkable consistency, the view which he had formed during the 1880's concerning the population problem and other social and religious questions. Nor did he cease propagating them. As late as 1924, for instance, he made a contribution to the population problem in which are found the same basic views as in his first sensational pamphlet. But now he no longer created any scandal, for in the meantime the popular viewpoint had shifted, and it could probably be shown that Wicksell's own persistent and sensational propaganda played a not unimportant role in this shift.

The

Introduction 5

A different view

The only economist who seems to have understood what Wicksell actually did in the field of poverty and population was Johan Åkerman. Quite probably this has to do with the fact that Åkerman was more of a 'broad' social scientist than a 'narrow,' technical economist. He was looking for other qualities in Wicksell's writings than the vast majority of his colleagues. In the first issue of *Econometrica*, Åkerman (1933: 114) provides the following summary evaluation of Wicksell's contribution to the theory of population:

> Wicksell is, perhaps, Malthus' most remarkable successor. What Wicksell said several decades ago regarding the necessity of restricting the increase of population – drawing on himself the persecution of conservative Society – is today generally accepted. His researches on marriage, birth, and death rates, and their economic and social consequences, opened up the possibility of calculating an optimum of population. At the present time, however, the population of the optimum is not the same as at the time of Knut Wicksell's researches. The conceptions of economic relativity and economic dynamics have modified the problem.
>
> Nevertheless, Wicksell gave to the theory of population a new impulse that proved to be of capital importance. He demonstrated that for every estimate of an optimum of population a thorough knowledge of the whole economic mechanism is essential. And as that mechanism is put in motion by human requirements and opinions with respect to the relative utility of everything that can satisfy these requirements, the theory of population must in the last instance rest on the theory of value.

The key phrase in the quotation from Åkerman is 'a thorough knowledge of the whole economic system is essential.' This is what the present work is about. We will present Wicksell's views of the causes of poverty, its consequences and remedy, as they appear in his writings, sprinkled with a liberal dose of quotations, in the hope of conveying at least some of the flavor of his unique – slightly involved – personal style of writing. It will then be argued that there is a great deal more originality in Wicksell than that which is commonly realized. Wicksell's views on population growth, diminishing returns and poverty, in fact, constitute a fully fledged general equilibrium system of international trade and migration (possibly also capital movements), along the lines that would be foreshadowed in the 1930s by Gottfried Haberler (1936), but formalized only by later international trade theorists, notably Ronald Jones (1971) and Paul Samuelson (1971a,b). It is mainly here, and less in his insistence on Malthusian characteristics or in his discussion of the optimum population, that Knut Wicksell's original contribution to the analysis of poverty and population lies. The optimum population concept is just one of many buildings blocks in Wicksell's system, and it is only when we take a comprehensive view of this system that his insistence on the optimum becomes fully intelligible.

We will start the story of Knut Wicksell's views of poverty and population in Chapter 2, with an account of how he began his neo-Malthusian career by delivering a speech at a temperance lodge in 1880 on the causes of drunkenness – an event that ended in a major public scandal, and which quite probably was instrumental when it came to turning Wicksell, who at the time was a mathematics student, into an economist. Chapter 3 is devoted to an account of Wicksell's longest piece on poverty and population, simultaneously his first attempt to produce a scientific essay on the subject. The occasion was a contribution to a French prize contest in 1891. The piece has fallen into almost complete oblivion because it has never been printed and appears to have been read by a mere handful of people in modern times. It is important because it offers a comprehensive and coherent view of Wicksell's thinking on the population problem. Had it been available to those in the economics profession, their verdict would possibly have been different.

In Chapter 4, we will turn to the centerpiece in all Wicksell's writings on population and poverty: diminishing returns to labor, not only in agriculture, where land was a fixed factor, but in the rest of the economy as well. We will then also deal with Wicksell's technological pessimism and sketch how he did not believe that technological progress could, in the longer run, neutralize and overcome the income-depressing effects of diminishing returns.

Directly related to diminishing returns is overpopulation. When the population grows rapidly, while the growth of output is held back by diminishing returns, the size of the population easily expands beyond what is optimal from the income point of view. Chapter 5 will relate how Wicksell thought that this stage had already been reached in Europe, including his own country, Sweden, and Germany. The chapter also shows that Wicksell considered that overpopulation would be conducive to war. Finally, it deals with the possibility of bridging the gap between population and income growth by resorting to specialization and international trade. Wicksell did not believe that this would solve the problem. Chapter 6, in turn, presents his views on emigration as a solution mainly of the past – a subject that he dealt with on various occasions.

With both international trade and emigration rendered ineffective, the problem of population and poverty remained, and Wicksell saw no other way of solving it than by reducing the size of the population until a stationary size was realized at the level that maximized per capita income. Chapter 7 deals with Wicksell's concept of optimum population and how he envisioned that the optimal state should be reached.

In Chapter 8 we will present a summary view of Wicksell's views of poverty and population growth, pulling together the evidence gathered in Chapters 2–7. We will use the stylized facts that emerge and synthesize these in a general equilibrium model of international trade between two 'large' regions: the Old World, i.e. Europe, and the New World, essentially the overseas regions of recent settlement. This model will be solved for the main parameter changes discussed by Wicksell in his writings, in order to show that Wicksell argued within the implicit framework of a remarkably modern, coherent general equilibrium system capable of handling all of his questions and worries.

Chapter 9, finally, raises an inevitable question: Why have Wicksell's works on population and poverty not received the attention and praise they rightly deserve? Why have his readers failed to perceive his originality in this area as well? We will seek the answers mainly in his fervent conviction and the circumstances surrounding the presentation and publication of his ideas.

With this, let us turn to Knut Wicksell's story. We will then begin with an account of his earliest public statement on poverty and population. This occasion is an important one, as there Wicksell gave vent to ideas that would stay with him for the rest of his life and make an imprint on everything he later said and wrote on the subject.

2 Tumultuous beginnings
The cause of poverty and its remedy

Knut Wicksell had begun his academic studies in the fall of 1869 with the firm proposition to get a PhD and possibly in the end also a professorial chair in mathematics. His bachelor's degree two and a half years later had included mathematics and astronomy, but also philosophy, history, Latin and Scandinavian languages (Gårdlund, 1996: 29). It was not until five or six years later that he began to display an interest in the social issues of the time. The circumstances were as follows.

As a young man, Wicksell had been religious, but during the course of the 1870s he gradually began to question his faith and instead began to look for a substitute that could serve as a guide in life. Under the influence of a student of medicine, Hjalmar Öhrvall, whose acquaintance he made in the fall of 1877, who had been a free-thinker since his teens, he began to look for an ideology 'that could be combined with the demands of truthfulness and utility' (Gårdlund, 1996: 45). In this process, the two friends stumbled across *The Elements of Social Science*, a book published anonymously in English in 1854, which appeared in Swedish in 1878 (Drysdale, 1878).[1] This book was to be published in no fewer than thirty-five English editions and ten editions in foreign languages (Gårdlund, 1979: 2). The Swedish edition had been translated from the sixteenth English one. Its author was the Scottish physician George Drysdale, whose identity, however, was not revealed until half a century after the publication of the work. The reading of this book would provide the most important input for all of Knut Wicksell's writings on poverty and population. Wicksell made Drysdale's ideas his own and never ceased to propagate them in his writings and public appearances. The book was nothing less than a revelation – a violent eye-opener – for him.

Wicksell's source of inspiration

Drysdale's book (Drysdale, 1876) is a curious mixture of medicine, religion and social issues. The first, short part deals with 'physical religion.'

Drysdale writes about men and women as physicians, about subjective medical science, life and death, the state of health in urban areas, spiritual illnesses and spiritualism. The second part, which is much more substantial, concentrates on 'sexual religion': mainly sexually transmitted diseases and other physical irregularities. The last sections, however, introduce the population problem along Malthusian lines. There, Drysdale points to Malthus' conclusions as incontrovertible – 'as conclusive as a problem of Euclid' (Drysdale, 1876: 272) – and states that he does not know of any work that is as important for the happiness of mankind as Malthus' (1989) *Essay on Population* (Drysdale, 1876: 273), the contents of which he presents thereafter in considerable detail. He ends his account on a euphoric note, which Wicksell would later echo (Drysdale, 1876: 315):

> . . . I cannot but consider its author to have been the greatest benefactor of mankind, *without any exception*, that ever existed on this earth. I do not say that Mr. Malthus possessed the greatest genius, or the most exalted moral character, that has appeared in history; but that the discovery of the law of population, which he made, and the service he thus rendered to his race was of a higher nature than any other ever conferred upon mankind. It is a discovery, which, in fact, stands quite alone and unapproachable among discoveries, in its relation to human happiness. Compared with it, the labours of poets, of a Shakespeare, a Voltaire, a Goethe, or a Byron; of the physical inquirers – as Newton, Laennec, Humboldt, or Bacon, are utterly insignificant in their power over human happiness. The law of population is beyond all comparison the most important law ever discovered, and the most indispensable contribution to moral, medical, and political science.

The presentation of the Malthusian doctrine is followed by a short account of John Stuart Mill's views of the economic consequences of population growth, as they appear in Book I of his *Principles of Political Economy*. This account culminates in a discussion of how the fixed character of the production factor land makes for diminishing returns in agriculture. Drysdale (1876: 318) quotes Mill (1929: 177) verbatim:

> 'This general law of agricultural industry', says Mr. Mill, 'is the most important proposition in political economy. Were the law different, nearly all the phenomena of the production and distribution of wealth would be other than they are. The most fundamental errors which still prevail on our subject, result from not perceiving this law at work underneath the more superficial agencies on which attention fixes itself.'

As we will find, below, this was to become the cornerstone in Wicksell's work on population.

The last and longest section in the second part, one of the sections that were to be of central importance for Wicksell, is labeled 'Poverty, Its Only Cause and Its Only Cure.' Drysdale opens his exposition by making it plain that the rich had never cared much about the fate of the poor; it was simply to work for the rich, and he poses the question of whether it would not have been better for them had they never been born. He argues that so far, in 'old countries' (Drysdale, 1876: 337), there had been no real human progress, and the reason for this was the excessive growth of the population: '. . . hitherto all happiness has been built on the misery of others' (Drysdale, 1876: 338). Competition among an excessive population had ensured that.

Drysdale argues against postponing the age of marriage, as suggested by Malthus, and instead makes a case for the use of contraceptive devices to limit the growth of the population. He argues that the use of contraceptives is 'the only possible way of introducing real morality into human society' (Drysdale, 1876: 352), because it prevents Malthus' 'positive' checks from coming into play. The non-satisfaction of the sexual drive was seen by him as something unnatural, conducive to bad health both for men and for women. The only way to obtain sexual satisfaction that was sanctioned by contemporary Victorian society was sex within the matrimony, but Drysdale attacks the institution of marriage, arguing that it 'spoils the social pleasures between the young of both sexes' (Drysdale, 1876: 356).

Drysdale considers it a duty to limit procreation. This is, however, difficult as long as the women are dependent on the men and hence have to marry. In order to make them more independent, Drysdale advocates higher wages for women (something that would inspire Wicksell to write a poem), but this is possible only if the rate of population growth declines and occupations so far closed for women are opened to them. Drysdale also attacks the hypocrisy attached to marriage. The fact that men are married does not put an end to fornication and prostitution. The only way to achieve that is to allow regular sexual intercourse outside the marriage. 'If young people could have a due amount of the sexual pleasures in an honourable and open way, without binding themselves down for life, mercenary and prostituted love would soon become extinct' (Drysdale, 1876: 369).

Drysdale wants to substitute a voluntary contract, agreed by two free parties, for marriage, 'so long as they love each other' (Drysdale, 1876: 371). He argues that the state should refrain altogether from defending the institution of matrimony and instead leave this to free, contracting parties whom should themselves agree on the conditions (Drysdale, 1876: 379-80). Wicksell would later both propagate and practice precisely this.

Part three, which is the shortest in the book, is about 'natural religion.' Part four, on the other hand, is again substantial. There, Drysdale spells out his complete social theory. The first sections concentrate on population growth, whereas the last sections are nothing but a summary of Mill's *Principles*. Drysdale sets up four laws that regulate human procreation. The first one states that whenever the population of a country grows at a rate below the maximum possible one, this depends on one or more of the following six factors: celibacy, prostitution, sterility, preventive sexual intercourse, premature death and emigration. Second, differences in population growth rates between countries are due to the same factors. Third, as a result of the existence of diminishing returns in agriculture the population cannot grow at the maximum possible rate; one or more of the six obstacles must come into play. Finally, emigration is not a permanent obstacle to population growth in a country, just an insignificant and temporary one. It can hence be deleted from the list of obstacles. Furthermore, Drysdale argues, the quantitative importance of sterility is so small that, in practice, this factor can be deleted too. Finally, the word 'poverty' can be substituted for 'premature death,' because it is the main cause of the latter. This leaves only celibacy, prostitution, preventive sexual intercourse and poverty as regulators of the size of the population.

In practice, according to Drysdale, the choice of means when it comes to limiting the size of the population is between preventive intercourse on the one hand and celibacy, prostitution and poverty on the other. However, 'Prolonged sexual abstinence is so intolerable an evil that it has never been borne alone but has always been found associated with the alternative evils of prostitution and poverty' (Drysdale, 1876: 466) This leaves only preventive intercourse.

Drysdale attempts to arrive at a quantitative idea of the relative importance of all the six factors, except infertility, in different countries. He then turns to the mechanism through which population growth causes poverty: the competition among too many workers that depresses the wage rate. Wages can rise if there is capital accumulation and technological progress resulting in capital formation, but if the population grows too fast, even so, wages will be kept down. It is not competition as such that serves to depress the wage rate but the excessive number of competitors in the labor market.

Drysdale thereafter again turns to diminishing returns in agriculture. These may in principle be mitigated or swamped by technological progress: 'an increase of agricultural skill, better means of conveyance by roads or railways, mechanical inventions which cheapen the tools used in husbandry, the application of machinery to the cultivation of the soil, or to the preparation of its products for human use' (Drysdale, 1876: 490), as well as the abolition of unfavorable institutions. However, writes Drysdale, echoing Mill, the point at which diminishing returns set in had already been reached, as less productive land was already being cultivated and the labor intensity of cultivation had increased. Both produce diminishing returns. The result of this was that the population had grown at a rate far below the maximum possible one. Still, the growth rate was too high, as witnessed by the existence of poverty.

Still, Drysdale argues, to abstain from sexual activity is not advisable. 'The Law of Exercise is that *the health of the reproductive organs and emotions depends on their having a sufficient amount of normal exercise*; and that a want of this tends powerfully to produce misery and disease in both man and woman' (Drysdale, 1876: 492). As Gårdlund (1996: 57) remarks, the latter was 'almost totally incorrect,' and only due to the insufficient knowledge about bacteriological diseases at the time. However, he writes, 'Drysdale's work contained also . . . [a] more reasonable idea' (Drysdale, 1876: 495):

> The sexual emotions are primarily excited by the formation and accumulation of the reproductive secretions: and they react upon the organs which prepare these secretions, directing towards them a current of blood and nervous influence, from which their nourishment is derived and their vigor supported. If the excitement be carried off by its natural channel, namely sexual union, the balance of health is maintained; if not, disorder of body and mind, varying in proportion to the strength of the arrested feelings and the susceptibility of the system, will result. According to the principle of the *composition of causes*, the emotion, though counteracted, still produces its full effect: but it operates now by deranging the other bodily and mental functions. Blushing, palpitation of the heart, hysterical convulsions, nervous irritability, and general disorder of the nutritive processes, are among the effects of repressed emotion, and consequently misdirected blood. The health of the mind suffers no less than that of the body. The will is rendered weak and irresolute by the conflict of the feelings: the thoughts are perturbed and the healthy links of association broken: restlessness, vehemence, anxiety, and hypochondria pervade the mind, and not unfrequently [*sic*] lead to confirmed insanity. Natural emotions, when unduly repressed, are as dangerous to the health of body and mind, as repressed secretions.

Drysdale provides three different sets of proofs for his thesis: physiological, pathological and therapeutical. The quotation belongs to the first category. The second category contains the mistaken views referred to by Gårdlund and the third line of proofs is concluded by a quotation from a leading contemporary medical authority: 'The more the function of an organ is used . . . the more it is nourished and the more it increases in size. Unless this physiological law be a dream, it must be applied to the genital organs' (Drysdale, 1876: 501).

A cause célèbre

As we will find on repeated occasions in the present work, Drysdale's work provided a constant source of inspiration for Wicksell's writings on population. Most immediately, his book, 574 pages in fine print, gave Wicksell the impulse for what would become his first, but in no way his last, cause célèbre. Knut Wicksell's entrance into the public debate was a behemoth one. It took place at the temperance lodge *Hoppets Här* (The Army of Hope) in Uppsala on 19 February 1880. The subject of Wicksell's talk was 'The Most Common Causes of Habitual Drunkenness and How to Remove Them.' He later published his lecture under the title *A Few Remarks on the Chief Cause of Social Misfortunes and the Best Means to Remedy Them, With Particular Reference to Drunkenness* (Wicksell, 1880a, 1999a).[2]

At that time Knut Wicksell was already known for radical views. During a reunion of Scandinavian students at Uppsala University in 1878, he had delivered the traditional 'Address to Woman,' an affair which in ninety-nine out of a hundred cases would result in a praise of her beauty and other conventional female virtues. Wicksell's case, however, was the hundredth (Gårdlund, 1990: 37–9). The poem he delivered on that occasion was anything but traditional. As Christina Jonung and Inga Persson (1997: 3–4) have perspicaciously observed, it anticipates Gary Becker's (1975) theory of marriage by almost a century. It refers to wealth as the traditional ornament of woman, argued that society was constructed in such a way as to make it impossible for women who were not rich to reach respected positions. It does not have much room for poverty-stricken seamstresses who would never attract wealthy admirers. Also, Wicksell, the poet, argues, women have smaller appetites than men and are therefore justly and wisely rewarded with lower wages. Finally, unequal access to human capital shapes the futures of men and women differently. Wicksell was looking forward to the day when marriage was contracted by means of free and equal contracts. All this was clearly inspired by his reading of Drysdale.

The poem had been published in the local Uppsala newspaper, but there was little in its contents that could have prepared the public for what was to come in February 1880. In his speech at the temperance lodge, Wicksell posed the question why people drink. His answer was that drunkenness is simply a symptom of poverty, and (Wicksell, 1999a: 86):

... when I say poverty I do not mean merely sheer, ragged destitution (this would still be limiting the concept unduly). No, I call any person poor who does not possess and has no reasonable prospect of acquiring what he direly needs. If the word is understood thus, I think that we will be forced to admit that the poor among us are not few, but legion.

Wicksell became very personal during his lecture. His vision of poverty and its consequences sprang directly from his own experience. He painted a vivid picture of a visit to a shoemaker (Wicksell, 1999a: 87):

When I opened the door to his abode, a dense white vapour at once gushed forth, and the air that met me was so very stifling and unwholesome that for a good while I really had to gasp for breath. When I finally plucked up courage and went in, I found before me a room not much larger than my own, small student's room, but literally packed full of people. In the middle of the floor, the master himself sat working with an apprentice, surrounded by as many of his numerous children as were not at school. Finally, at the stove, his wife was busy with a couple of other women working on a large mass of boiled sugar, of which they were to make Danish caramels for sale; and I assure you, ladies and gentlemen, the strong smell of burnt sugar, combined with an equally strong stench of wet leather, particularly when supplemented by the inevitable odour given off by so many people, made up a total impression to which my nose, at least, was insufficiently inured. I therefore hurried as fast as I could to complete my business and get away from there, but the memory I took with me I will not forget so easily. And yet what I had seen was by no means extreme or unusual distress, but merely plain, common poverty.

Wicksell posed the rhetorical question whether, under these circumstances, one should be surprised, 'even for a moment' (Wicksell, 1999a: 87), if the shoemaker escaped from his home in order to get drunk in a tavern – 'a veritable paradise compared with *his* abode' (Wicksell, 1999a: 87). Of course not. Poverty alone, Wicksell suggested, was more than enough to 'explain the increasing tendency toward the excesses of drunkenness and other debauchery that marks the youth of our times' (Wicksell, 1999a: 91).

But, said Wicksell, poverty had not been man's eternal companion, and there was a remedy for it. In order to understand what the proper remedy is, it was, however, necessary to be familiar with 'the view of the causes of poverty that is named after the English clergyman and economist Malthus', because through his profound studies of the question he provided 'once and for all' (Wicksell, 1999a: 95) the firm foundation that the theory has to build on. Wicksell (1999a: 95) summarized Malthus' views:

> In every country of old cultivation, the population, if left to itself, has a natural tendency to grow at a far more rapid rate than the means of subsistence. The consequence of this is poverty with its customary attendants, vice and crime, and although it can by no means be claimed that these misfortunes derive from overpopulation alone, all means to remedy them will nevertheless prove powerless unless population growth is *regulated* at the same time, in such a way that the development of the food supply can keep pace with it.

Inspired, no doubt, by his reading of Drysdale, Wicksell was completely convinced that the Malthusian population theory is a physical law. 'In spite of innumerable ferocious attacks,' he wrote, 'the "law of population" remains as unrefuted as a mathematical theorem' (Wicksell, 1999a: 96). To allege that a country could not become overpopulated amounted to nonsense.

Wicksell went very far in his stress of the negative effects of population growth. He claimed that (Wicksell, 1999a: 99):

> . . . there is not a single important event in history that is not incompletely explained if this weighty factor has been neglected, not a single one of the most terrifying scenes of ancient times that does not emerge into a truer and at the same time more human light, if it is seen from the light of impending overpopulation.

Of course, nature itself possesses a number of remedies against overpopulation, but these are of the negative kind, like, for example, diseases and starvation. 'In China, the most fertile land on earth, but equally proverbial for its population density, famine is now said to be – permanent' (Wicksell, 1999a: 101). Above all, human societies had resorted to war. Wicksell's comment is cynical (Wicksell, 1999a: 101):

> Now it is no doubt true that the relief war brings is not felt immediately, since of course some of those whose labour would otherwise support the rest of the population are lost in the war; the relief only comes somewhat later, when those who are thus left without a provider have had the time to starve to death.

Wicksell was careful to point out that the alternative to war, 'that human societies have employed, though far more sparingly than the previous expedient, and usually in combination with it, has been emigration'

(Wicksell, 1999a: 101). In the end, however, the difference may not be too important, for those who emigrate are men and women in their most productive age, and those left behind are 'those who are infirm and unfit for work' (Wicksell, 1999a: 102). Another remedy was infanticide, common during earlier historical periods, and still practiced among 'savage and semi-civilized peoples' (Wicksell, 1999a: 102), and the priests of the Catholic church practiced celibacy.

Wicksell moved on to discuss contemporary remedies. The majority of the male population hardly considered celibacy an alternative. Instead, the 1880s had '*poverty, late marriages, drunkenness, prostitution* and secret *infanticide*' (Wicksell, 1999a: 104). The last, of course, was prohibited in Sweden, but there was little that the authorities could do if poor women chose to let their infants starve to death. The law, in other words, by and large remained a dead letter. The alternative was clear to Wicksell (1996: 106):

> If . . . we desire not merely to forbid infanticide on paper, as is now done, but actually to prevent it, if we desire to protect these little ones from sufferings they have done nothing to deserve, then there is only one means to this end, and as long as human beings are human beings there will be but a single means: and this is to make it possible for every mother to give birth to and bring up at least one or two children, in honour and decency.

Wicksell recommended a slow population growth (something that he would later give up in favor of a stationary population). In his contemporary Sweden, the average number of children per family was four or five, which he thought was far too many. Even with three children who would reach adult age, the Swedish population would continue to grow. With two, on the other hand, it would shrink slightly, so (Wicksell, 1999a: 106):

> . . . the one correct average compatible with a *healthy* increase in the population must be found somewhere between two and three, and in future we must strive to meet this goal, if we are to have any hope of permanent relief from poverty and all social misery.

The alternative was out of question (Wicksell, 1999a: 107):

> . . . what of the Swedish cottar, the impoverished Swedish labourer, who sees himself surrounded in his hovel by his five or six – indeed, up to eight or ten – children, for whose future he is generally unable to make the least provision, and of whom, perhaps not he himself, but

anyone else can confidently predict that at least one of the sons will be impelled by *necessity* to become a beggar and a drunkard, at least one of the daughters will be forced by *necessity* to take up the most ignominious, the most unhappy of livelihoods. What *he* thinks, I do not know, and I would like to assume, for the sake of his honour, that he has not devoted much thought to the matter.

Wicksell (1999a: 108) concluded:

> *Therefore, once their eyes have been opened to these facts, every married couple ought to regard it as a sacred duty, indeed, as the most sacred of all duties, not to increase their family to more than two or three children without careful consideration.*

This, however, might be next to impossible without proper, professional assistance. Having reached this point in his lecture, Wicksell completed the public scandal, by entering a subject 'which at that time could scarcely be mentioned between husband and wife or among friends' (Gårdlund, 1996: 45–6). He openly recommended the use of contraceptive devices to limit the growth of the population, and not only that, but he also suggested that the medical profession should assist without hesitation in the effort (Wicksell, 1999a: 108):

> If there is therefore any means, if doctors, guided by their science, are able to indicate any way of making his duty, for some, less burdensome, for others, perhaps, possible to fulfil at all, in other words, some way of making conjugal relations possible without the woman becoming pregnant – then in truth, they ought to hasten in this case, too, to place their knowledge in the service of suffering humanity. They ought to do this without regard to such prejudices as have always opposed every beneficial innovation, every new blessing for the human race, but in support of which, as *they* should be in the position to judge, not a single reason, ethical, rational or religious, can ultimately be advanced.

The reaction

Wicksell repeated his lecture less than a week later, on 25 February 1880, this time in front of an audience consisting mainly of his fellow students and academic teachers at Uppsala University. He exhorted them to form societies that could propagate the idea that contraceptives should be used. He was greeted with ovations – but not by everybody. A number of pamphlets were written in which his views were condemned (e.g. Cornelius, 1880;

Hamilton, 1880; Hammarskjöld, 1880; Jönsson, 1880; Lindblom, 1880), not least by the Uppsala Medical Association (Åberg *et al.*, 1880), which had no intention whatsoever of heeding his call for information, and he received an admonition by the Lower University Council at Uppsala.[3] No wonder: he had broken a taboo in late nineteenth-century Oscarian Sweden. 'And taboo limits were something under which Knut Wicksell neither then nor later in his life could resist putting a little load of gunpowder' (Nordqvist, 1985: 60).

The Council was especially upset by the fact that Wicksell, during the second of his lectures, had argued that he considered 'no place, not even the pulpit itself, to be too exalted for the preaching of these doctrines' (Wicksell, 1999a: 110), and one of the points it made was that Wicksell, 'before appearing in public with exhortations to resort to measures that interfere deeply with family life' had not undertaken 'even moderately extensive studies in the science – economics – that . . . [he wanted] to use as his point of departure' (Åberg *et al.*, 1880: 119–20). In this, it was backed by the leading Swedish economist at the time, David Davidson, then *docent* (associate professor) in economics at Uppsala University (Wicksell, 1880a: 79–94).[4]

Formally, the critics were right, because Wicksell's only exposure to Malthus' ideas at the time when he gave his two lectures and wrote his pamphlet was through Drysdale (Kock, 1944: 84; Gårdlund, 1996: 54), and he had not yet begun his studies in economics. Possibly (and perhaps even probably), as Wicksell's granddaughter Liv Wicksell Nordqvist (1985: 62) has remarked in her biography of Wicksell's wife Anna Bugge, Davidson's (and the other critics') accusation was one of the reasons why Knut Wicksell, once he had finished his *licentiat* degree in mathematics and physics in 1885, chose to switch to economics. According to Emil Sommarin (1926–7: 24), Wicksell's successor as professor of economics at Lund University, Wicksell 'had with a light irony hinted that there was always something for which he could be grateful to his often not too loyal adversaries.'

Moral, or rather moralistic, arguments were not lacking either. The foremost custodian of moral values among Wicksell's critics was the young Boströmian philosopher[5] from Uppsala, Lawrence Heap Åberg, who threw the rights of the unborn into Wicksell's face (Wicksell, 1880: 76–8; English translation in Gårdlund, 1996: 61):

[The carnal gospel that we yesterday heard preached][6] give men an opportunity for pleasure, pleasure for which the offspring must be sacrificed; but it shall die without pain, its parents' joy shall not be spoiled by any grating cries. No, their offspring's death is nothing but a source of pleasure, reckless pleasure. Never-ending would be the immorality ensuing from the practical application of his doctrine. And yet it would be perpetrated within the bounds of marriage. One of Society's most holy institutions would thus be transformed into an image of Moloch, in whose shadow the tares of lust would flourish freely. Or has not Herr W. realized that in this way he will transform marriage into prostitution, which we know he abhors? He drags what is holy into the dust and takes us back to the worship of Baal. And in the arms of lust the disciples will cry aloud, 'Baal, hear us!'

Wicksell, however, had his sympathizers too. Perhaps the most ardent one was a French feminist, Augustine Descard, working in Sweden as a French teacher, who wrote a few passionate letters to him – letters that come dangerously close to love letters – after having read his pamphlet (Hashimoto, forthcoming, Letter 1):

> They are accusing you, because they do not understand you, or they are not looking enough for the meaning of your ideas. Man has his principles and more or less old prejudices. So what . . . Your thoughts are noble, and those who attack you are far from arousing the same interest as you.

Reading the pamphlet by Åberg *et al*., Descard had taken special offense by what David Davidson had written about how population growth was being limited in her native country (Hashimoto, forthcoming, Letter 2):

> Mr. Davidson describes the French laws in a way that is so far from the truth that I have asked a doctor among these friends to tell him that he has given proof of gross ignorance by saying that infanticide was practiced by surgeons who make a fortune from it and that this crime is tolerated by the law. If Mr. Davidson had read our laws he would have seen that this crime is punished by 20 years of forced labor. His discourse strongly resembles that of an idiot, and if it had not been so false, I would have believed him to be malicious. He is stupid, that's all, but, frankly speaking, that's enough.

The end of the letter reads almost like a proposition, especially considering that Augustine had urged Wicksell to travel incognito to Stockholm 'for a few hours,' as 'if I am not mistaken, I sense that you are unhappy':

> There is nothing offensive in your book, but actually there is a reasoning that I do not understand, when it comes to preventive devices [;] it seems to me that love has been put a little on the side in order to make

room for a realism that cannot exist, as I see it, either between lovers or between newly-weds, but I will not elaborate any more on this subject. Thus, I will not tell you why this does not seem in fact intelligible, or even natural. I will tell you if you come to Stockholm, and I really hope that that you will be nice enough to do me that favor, I will be at home all day. It would be much easier to write to each other when we have met and you have got to know me a little better.

At this point it is getting very late. I have to say good night to you and until next time. Be convinced that I will not forget you and that my correspondence with you will be my most precious pastime.

Toward the end of 1880, Wicksell responded to his critics in great detail (Wicksell, 1880a: 71–95; 1880b). Gårdlund (1996: 54) makes the conjecture that essentially his first lecture had been 'a brilliant improvisation.' The entire contents had been based on Drysdale. Possibly, Wicksell underestimated the feelings that it would arouse (Gårdlund, 1996: 47). At any rate, the lectures and the pamphlet brought pandemonium, and he could not let the critics have the last word. Accordingly, Wicksell sat down and penetrated the population question. Davidson, who in due course would become a close friend, had lent him his own, personal copy of Malthus (Uhr, 1962: 4). In his response, Wicksell, however, deals mainly with points related to social medicine and less with the economic aspects (Gårdlund, 1996: 66).

With this response, Wicksell had chosen to become deeply involved in a debate that would occupy him for the rest of his life. His speeches and two pamphlets had provided the foundations for all his further writings on poverty and population growth. There was no question in Wicksell's mind. The latter caused the former, and the only way to reduce poverty went through early marriages between spouses that had been educated with respect to the use of contraceptive devices that could be used to limit the size of their families and hence also of the total population. Only then would it be possible to raise the incomes and living standards of the population in general.

There was no way back for Wicksell. Two years later, he published another major pamphlet that dealt with population growth: *Om utvandringen, dess betydelse och orsaker* [*On Emigration: Its Importance and Causes*].[7] Another four years later, in December 1886, Wicksell was deeply involved in the international neo-Malthusian movement. In a letter to the editor of *The Malthusian*, published in early 1887, Charles R. Drysdale, the brother of George Drysdale, wrote (Hashimoto, forthcoming, Letter 12):

You will be glad to hear that I have begun this winter a little propagandist work in Stockholm. I have given, and am still giving, some popular lectures (about once a week) on several topics, economical and moral, but all with the intention of showing how the population question lies at the very root of nearly all the social phenomena. Hitherto I have had good audiences, and have met with rather friendly criticisms in the papers, although none of the leading journals show any marked sympathy with Malthusianism. On the contrary, they all seem to think that we could maintain a much larger population in Sweden if only 'our slumbering millions' (meaning some hidden treasures in the ground) could be utilised, 'the spirit of enterprise' be aroused, and so on. In the meantime, emigration is going on at a considerable rate; and the growth of our foreign debt is becoming a most serious affair. And to think that people hope to cure these evils – by putting a duty on wheat and rye! The 'fair trade' movement here seems to make great progress, especially amongst our country population.

My friends and I earnestly think of forming a Swedish Malthusian League. Perhaps the work will be more successful when carried out with united forces.

Before this, however, Wicksell had turned to serious studies of economics. In 1885, he had left Sweden for London, where he spent most of his time at the British Museum, penetrating the classic and contemporary economic literature, and in the evenings he visited the radical political English scene, notably the Fabian Society, but he did not discard other points of view either, although when it came to the population issue his ideas had already been formed (Gårdlund, 1990: 86–7):

On Thursday I was debating with anarchists. Kautsky and I cannot fully understand another. He is saying that Malthusianism is only a psychological, not a social, question. When I am pressing him, he says that all will come by itself, when once the socialist question is settled, and that it is not wise for the Socialists to split their forces on several things at the time. I think that the fault is, that he has gone to the subject in a historical way only, whereas I think you must be accustomed with mathematics before, at the least so much as to be fully at home in the axiomas [*sic*] of algebra.

After returning from London in 1886, Wicksell devoted a great deal of his time to lecturing in various Scandinavian cities on a number of subjects, most of which were related to the population question: the population question itself, prostitution, marriage, and euthanasia. As we will see below, he would again offend the conservative moral, and with that its worldly representatives, notably those in uniform. In the middle of the turmoil that he caused, however, his views continued to be cemented. In May 1888, when Wicksell was in Vienna attending economics lectures by Carl Menger, Lujo Brentano and Isidor Singer, he wrote back home to one of his most intimate friends, Theodor Frölander, about how he was looking for a subject to write on. The topic had to fall within population theory, and it should not be too narrowly specified (Gårdlund, 1996: 111):

> But a work that is needed, is some sort of continuation of Malthus: a detailed account of the increase of the population in Europe during this century and its distribution over the various . . . [professions], together with its causes and effects; also a complementary account of America's economic life and a prognosis of the future with a definite Malthusian twist at the end. A work of this kind would answer an urgent need and it would benefit *all* parties, but I am afraid that it would be *far* beyond my powers, at any rate for the moment, and it may be quite impracticable. However, I shall talk to Singer about it. Incredible that practically nothing has been written on this subject nowadays (Rümelin has stopped writing), but presumably people shrink from the unpleasant consequences.

Despite his misgivings, it would not take much more than a year before Wicksell set out to tackle the subject that he had sketched in his letter.

3 The causes of population growth

The French prize essay[1]

Knut Wicksell's lecture at *Hoppets Här* had pointed unequivocally to population growth as the cause of poverty, but, excepting the references to Malthus, it had not dwelt in any detail on what made the population grow. Ten years after the speech, however, Wicksell, who by then was an advanced student of economics, had an occasion to produce a more scientific piece on the economics of population growth. Despite the fact that it is completely central among his writings on population, this essay has remained unpublished and untranslated, so we will devote some space to a scrutiny of its contents.

At the beginning of July 1889, Wicksell had arrived in Paris as part of the European study tour that had also involved, among other things, his visit to Vienna. In October, he wrote back home to a friend that the Académie des sciences morales et politiques de l'Institut de France in Paris had advertised a competition for the 1891 Prix Rossi on the subject *La population, les causes de ses progrès et les obstacles qui en arrêtent l'essor* (Population, the causes of its progress and the obstacles that prevent its growth). Essays were due at the end of 1890, and Wicksell had decided to take part in the competition, spurred presumably both by his strong interest in the subject and his notoriously bad finances. The prize sum was 5,000 francs (Gårdlund, 1996: 124, 150).

Faithful to his ideals, Wicksell chose to tackle the subject in a neo-Malthusian fashion. He was the only one of the thirteen competitors who did so (Gårdlund, 1996 : 151). His essay (Wicksell, 1891) contained four chapters: one on the doctrine of Malthus and the criticism against it, one on the growth of the European population in the nineteenth century, one on the optimal population and, finally, one on the future population of Europe.

In his introduction to the essay, Wicksell noted that the formulation of the proposed theme seemed to exclude anything but a positive interpretation of population growth. Of course, he does not agree. On the contrary: the proposition has to be submitted to 'a rigorous examination' (Wicksell,

1891: 12). Wicksell proposed to investigate two issues: (i) Under which circumstances is population growth desirable, if so, which are the best ways to obtain it, and if not, how should a stationary or falling population be obtained?; and (ii) Given the economic conditions prevailing in a country, which is the most desirable number of inhabitants?

The Malthusian message

In the first chapter, Wicksell summarized Malthus' writings on population in five points:

(i)   The human race has an immanent tendency to reproduce, which is so strong that, if it is not checked, it will outstrip the growth of food production.
(ii) Thus, such checks must exist, because you never observe reproduction at the maximum possible rate.
(iii) These checks either operate on the birth rates or on the death rates. Also, emigration must be added to the picture.
(iv) It is desirable that forces reducing birth rates are substituted for forces increasing death rates.
(v)   A limitation of the birth rate ought thus to be 'a constant preoccupation for all the civilized peoples' (Wicksell, 1891: 37).

The first, central, Malthusian proposition Wicksell, exactly like Drysdale, regarded as a discovery 'of the same order and almost of the same nature as that of Newton' (the law of gravitation) (Wicksell, 1891: 40). He, however, took issue with the two celebrated rates of progression. As far as the geometric one for population is concerned, he states that it was far more important to get an idea about the *actual* rate of growth than about the maximum possible one. His objections to the second one were more serious. Wicksell, the mathematician, observed that the assumption of an arithmetic progression of the food supply was unrealistic, as the constancy of the difference between the terms of the series implied a falling *rate* of growth over time, to the point where in the end it would be infinitesimal. Besides, no arithmetic growth rate of food had ever been verified. '[T]his tour de force of the young author' (Malthus) of comparing the two series, 'is, in short, not very scientific' (Wicksell, 1891: 46). It was only when food production grows in geometric progression as well that the population could do so. Otherwise some check on the growth of the latter would immediately set in. Wicksell (1891: 47–8) concluded his criticism:

Thus, one actually finds oneself always at the very point of departure and the only problem consists in the reconciliation of the *present* tendency of population growth with the possibility of making the means of subsistence grow *at present* or in the immediate future. In other words, the formidable divergence of the two series will never occur, cannot occur; it is always with the two first terms in each of the two series that one actually has to do; but precisely, in Malthus' formula, these two terms are always the same in both series.

Wicksell argued that what Malthus actually was after was the existence of diminishing returns to labor, i.e. what Malthus himself had applied in his discussion of the formation of agricultural rent. Each term in the series for the progression of food production must be affected by diminishing returns. This idea, which he had come across through his reading of Drysdale, was of fundamental importance for Wicksell, and in Chapter 4 we will come back to how he, on various occasions, made it central in his discussion of poverty and population growth.

According to Wicksell, the only conclusion that can be drawn from Malthus' two famous series was that the means of subsistence cannot double every twenty-five years – 'something that is almost self-evident' (Wicksell, 1891: 51). What the maximum rate of procreation of humans may be, remained a largely unstudied question. Wicksell discussed the empirical examples of the United States agricultural frontier and Hungary, as well as some general population statistics, in order to get some empirical underpinning and concluded that Malthus' assertion that the size of a population may double in twenty-five years under favorable circumstances did not seem to be exaggerated. Maybe the figure should be put lower yet.

With regard to the desirability of influencing birth rates instead of death rates, Wicksell noted, a frequently stated objection was that the reduction of birth rates was in itself a costly sacrifice, but he argued that this was more than compensated for by a higher living standard. The main point, however, is that children are not born only because the parents so intend. There are other forces at work, notably the sexual instinct, and repressing that is costly. Malthus only recommended moral restraint (late marriages) but for Wicksell this represented 'a truly superhuman effort' (Wicksell, 1891: 23). 'To arrive at an equilibrium, or almost, between births and deaths, if the latter are reduced to their smallest possible figure, from the physiological point of view, would require that marriages were only celebrated between old maids and old men' (Wicksell, 1891: 111). Chastity within matrimony, in turn, was a little researched area and almost hopeless to discuss, as many people would even consider it obscene.

The growth of the European population

The second chapter of the prize essay dealt with population growth in Europe. Wicksell examined the causes of this growth and posed the question of whether the prevailing growth trend could be sustained. He rejected the frequently adduced argument that the growth rate should be considered low and contended that for five or six decades it had been too fast in most of Europe.

The reason for this excessive population growth was to be found in the growth of agricultural output over a hundred-year period as a result of scientific progress and institutional change. During that time, European agriculture had been transformed by the employment of crop rotation, chemical fertilizer, etc. Still, an output that was twice as high as the one at the beginning of the nineteenth century did not suffice. Europe had also had to resort to imports of foodstuffs from overseas. In great technical detail, Wicksell argued against those contending that substituting horticulture for agriculture, i.e. intensifying production, would help sustaining high population growth in the future. He did not consider that the success of this type of agriculture would be guaranteed by higher future population densities. On the contrary, when the population grew, the only ones to gain were the landowners, as rents would increase while wages would fall across the board. He definitely believed that at the beginning of the 1890s Europe was close to the point where no more progress would be possible in agriculture.

That left imports. Many of Wicksell's contemporary economists had argued that Europe should concentrate on the production of manufactures and resort to imports of foodstuffs. Wicksell found this worrying as all of the countries of Europe (with the possible exception of Russia) would soon be industrialized and hence would have to import at least one-half of their annual wheat consumption from overseas. That would lead to an impossible situation as the transoceanic producers would not be able to respond to this level of demand, because it would be impossible both to produce in Europe all the industrial goods that imports of this magnitude would require and because the requirements in terms of transportation would be beyond anything that would be practically possible. The overseas agricultural lands were no longer virgin. The frontier was closing rapidly. In addition, the demand for food was on the rise in these countries and they were also endeavoring to foster domestic industrial sectors, frequently behind tariff walls that made exports from the Old World difficult. For this they were not to be blamed, Wicksell said, as countries where the only employment is found in agriculture and possibly one or two extractive industries 'necessarily remain semi-barbarian' (Wicksell, 1891: 182). It was obviously not only Marx who was convinced of the idiocy of rural life.[2]

Wicksell posed the question of what would happen if the United States would lower its tariffs on manufactured goods. This would lead to a reduction of industrial wages and a transfer of workers into agriculture, where the wage rate would decline as well, whereas the landowners would benefit from increased land rents. Of course the price of manufacturing imports would decline but this would not necessarily compensate for the effect of the wage reduction.

Wicksell did not believe that specialization could continue. Assume that the Americas and other overseas primary producers would continue to supply Europe with grain while Europe would produce ten times as much industrial goods as hitherto, becoming the only producer of manufactures in the world. Would the latter be possible from the point of view of natural resource availability? Wicksell doubted it. The availability of coal for fuel and heating would not suffice. In the long run, declining coal production would act as a brake on the expansion of manufacturing. In Britain, the peak of industrial development had probably already been reached, and in the rest of Europe expansion was likely to be even more difficult. Procuring coal overseas would be out of question for transport reasons, and no serious attempt had been made to replace coal by other sources of energy.

Wicksell finished his second chapter with some remarks on emigration. That Europe could continue to increase its population because the surplus could always find an outlet in emigration overseas is a false argument. The scope for receiving further people in the new countries was limited. In particular it could not be expected that North America could continue to absorb the surplus population of Europe, of about three million people per annum. Thus, the only possible conclusion was that the doctrine of Malthus was confirmed.

The optimum population

This conclusion brought Wicksell into the topic of Chapter 3: 'The Optimum Number of Population.'[3] The population increase in Europe was not matched by scientific and industrial progress. It was doubtful whether during the twentieth century economic development in general could continue at the same pace as during the nineteenth. Quoting Paul Leroy-Beaulieu, Wicksell pointed out that there are three ways to use productivity increases: more leisure, higher consumption or more children. If the population increase was a result of a conscious choice, there would be no want of other goods. But this was precisely the point. The population increase was *not* the result of deliberate decisions.

The differences in living standards in Europe were a result mainly of the 'superabundance of population' (Wicksell, 1891: 238). Based on Malthus,

Ricardo had formulated the iron law of wages: the wage rate would not move above the level necessary for bare survival, as long as population growth was rapid. The only way to break away from this situation was by limiting the growth of the population. In Britain, trade unions had been able to push up the wage level by limiting entry to the labor market, but this would hardly be possible in the long run, should the population continue to grow. Competition between the workers would serve to bring the wage rate back to the subsistence level. Diminishing returns prevailed in manufacturing, and, unless counteracted by technological progress, this situation would continue. The wage would always be determined by the productivity of the last worker to be hired. The same principle applied in agriculture. In the new countries, the yield per hectare was usually lower than in the Old World, but the product per worker was higher. Thus wages were higher and rents lower than in Europe, where a 'flourishing' agricultural sector could only be bought at the price of low wages. It was only by limiting their numbers that the workers could push up the wage level.

Wicksell presented his idea of how this should be accomplished. It was not a satisfactory state of affairs that the supply of workers was regulated simply by the sexual instincts of the laboring classes. 'The heedless satisfaction of the sexual desire: will that for ever be the last word of our civilization in these questions?' (Wicksell, 1891: 282). In the introduction to his essay, he had defined the optimal population (without using the term): 'The number of inhabitants that is most desirable is, in our view, the one according to which the large mass of the population will live, above all materially speaking, in the most favorable situation' (Wicksell, 1891: 16). He hastened to point out that the normal condition of a people is that of stationariness or at least fluctuations around a certain equilibrium. This calls for an equilibrium between birth and death rates – the real population principle, which no historical epoch has been able to escape.

Wicksell argued that if it can be arranged that children are born only as a result of the rational conviction of their parents, they will find their place in the world without problems. The optimum population will then come about automatically. For Europe, that would imply a decreasing population everywhere. The opposition to this proposal would be found mainly among the upper classes, for it is not possible to have a leisure class in a situation where labor is scarce, only when it is abundant and has few, if any, alternatives.[4]

The future of Europe

The final chapter of the prize essay dealt with the future population of Europe. It was necessary to reduce its size, and if mortality would come down, so must nativity. The exaggerated mortality in Europe was due to poverty and ignorance, notably poverty. 'This will have to change, as quickly as possible, or our entire civilization will be a mere delusion' (Wicksell, 1891: 314). By the same token, however, birth rates had to be reduced to the corresponding extent. On average, what was required, was to cut nativity to about one-third of the actual European figure. This, Wicksell (1891: 320) stated, is 'the definitive conclusion' of his investigation (Wicksell, 1891: 319):

> Once this state of mortality has been regulated the stability of the population will be established again, arguably on a less dense scale, but also on a generally much higher level of prosperity that is generally much higher than that of our days.

There was only one way of arriving at the optimal population. The way advocated by Malthus himself, postponing marriage for a couple of years, would not suffice. 'In the light of modern statistics this assertion is of an almost ridiculous naïveté' (Wicksell, 1891: 326). What was needed was the neo-Malthusian, not the original Malthusian, solution.[5]

Wicksell's prize essay challenged Malthus in important respects, notably the theoretical and empirical relevance of the two celebrated series. In the essay he also discussed the problems related to specialization, international trade, and emigration: all important building blocks in what we will argue constitutes a coherent approach to the problem of poverty. Finally, the concept of optimum population and the extent to which the optimum had been exceeded in his contemporary Europe was dealt with in some detail.

At this point, we know what Wicksell considered to be the driving force behind the growth of the population and how population growth in turn leads to poverty. With this, let us turn to a more systematic examination of the rest of the building blocks of his theory. We will then begin with the pivotal part: diminishing returns.

4 The centerpiece of Wicksell's theory
Diminishing returns

The centerpiece of Knut Wicksell's writings on population growth and poverty is diminishing returns. Had it not been for diminishing returns, the population problem would have been much easier to solve but, as diminishing returns prevail everywhere in the economy, there is an inexorable tendency for population growth to result in a reduction of per capita income and wages. Wicksell was completely convinced that these diminishing returns were strong enough to swamp the productivity-increasing effects of technological progress in the long run. Not only that, but in his *Lectures in Political Economy* he wrote (Wicksell, 1934: 214):

> The unprecedented growth of the population recently witnessed in Europe, and still more in some extra-European countries, will certainly, sooner or later – probably in the course of the present century – prepare the way for much slower progress and possibly for completely stationary conditions.

At the core of this gloomy prediction we find the notion of diminishing returns.

The Swedish problem

On several occasions, Knut Wicksell gave voice to his pessimism with respect to the ability of the Swedish economy to increase production. He did not see as sustainable the 'extraordinary material progress' that Sweden as well as 'the civilized world in general' (Wicksell, 1887a: 22) had experienced during the preceding century. Agriculture could expand only slowly and the output of forest and iron products could not increase at rates equal to those of the past. Wicksell saw diminishing returns setting in everywhere. He did not hesitate in his discussion of the remedy. If income could not be made to expand fast enough, expenditures had to be reduced. 'It is possible, at least within certain limits, to live as happily with smaller incomes as with larger; it is simply a matter of adhering to the proverb; adjust the mouth – that is, the number of mouths – to the food bag' (Wicksell, 1887a: 24).

In his discussion of population growth and agriculture, Wicksell was more of a classical economist than a neoclassic. The mechanism he envisaged is familiar (Wicksell, 1892: 309):

> If, following a too strong population increase, production is displaced to ever more barren tracts, it will not only be the 'pioneers on the frontier of cultivation' that will suffer, but the entire labor force. Wages will fall across the board, in analogy with the simple hydrostatic law of communicating vessels. At the same time, the capitalist class is granted a favor, as unwarranted as it is shocking for the sense of justice and the requirements of humanitarianism, because of the glaring opposition between superabundance on the one hand and destitution on the other.

In 1914, the Swedish National Statistical Office published figures that indicated that fertility might be on decline in Sweden, and the daily newspaper *Dagens Nyheter* commented that this gave rise to 'serious misgivings.' In a comment on this article in a pamphlet, Wicksell (1914) quickly recapitulated his views on the population question, argued that *Dagens Nyheter* was completely mistaken and went on to discuss the fixed character of land. Production in agriculture can always be increased by increasing the capital stock and the number of workers, but '*never in full proportion to the increases of labor and capital themselves*' (Wicksell, 1914: 4). Increasing the population leads to a decline of the wage rate, whereas land rents and the return to capital increase. To some extent diminishing returns to labor may be counteracted by an increasing division of labor, but Wicksell thought that this factor was far more important in regions of recent cultivation than in Europe. He also contrasted agricultural labor productivity in extensively cultivated Argentina with intensively cultivated Sweden, referring the difference precisely to diminishing returns to labor.

Two years later, Wicksell (1958a) took issue with an article by Curt Rohtlieb (1916). Rohtlieb had argued that any law of agricultural returns must be of a technical or scientific kind and that as the classical economists who first formulated the law of diminishing returns had a very imperfect knowledge of the physical and chemical forces at play in agriculture, they may have been mistaken in their insistence on diminishing returns. An indignant Wicksell refuted the idea by a simple demonstration using a linearly homogeneous production function: '. . . if the statement is intended to mean that the critical point at which the law of agricultural returns begins to be valid has not yet been reached in Sweden, it is quite absurd, for this point was certainly passed some hundreds or even thousands of years ago' (Wicksell, 1958a: 134–5). He concluded his article by stating that the law of diminishing returns is no 'technical' question but 'entirely a matter of political economy, or rather, population' (Wicksell, 1958a: 137).

Wicksell emphasized the importance of diminishing returns in various contexts and expended a considerable effort on explaining it. In a discussion of an article on Malthusianism by Pontus Fahlbeck (1902), professor of political science in Lund, who was worried that a mere two children per family would lead to underpopulation or 'national suicide' and not increased national prosperity, Wicksell pointed out that diminishing returns to labor in agriculture had been reached long ago (Wicksell, 1902: 548), and stressed that diminishing returns are present in other branches as well (Wicksell, 1902: 548–9):

> Our economic development since the 1860s has essentially been *abnormal*; it has not been by a harmonious development of all our industries, with agriculture in the vanguard, but by a one-sided, ever more intensive elaboration of a few of these, especially our wood and partially also our iron industry that we have been able to procure employment and bread for so many people. Both these industries, however, unfortunately belong to the class of extractive industries; they allow a strong momentary flourishing, as has actually been the case, but in the long run it is impossible to live on them. How much is left before the bottom of our ore fields is reached is, however, still uncertain, but in our forest supply and hence in our iron-refining industry, we have already begun to see the bottom . . .

In his French prize essay, Wicksell (1891: 41) had dealt with England's problem of securing a coal production that would allow industrial output to grow in the future as well. As we saw in Chapter 3, he argued that the peak had already been reached. Sweden, he contended, was in equally bad shape, if not worse. In a lecture given in Oslo in 1907, he characterized the Swedish manufacturing sector as a 'house of cards' (Gårdlund, 1996: 258). As it was based on timber, the excessive felling would soon leave it without raw materials.

Of course, the capital stock could be increased, but given the capital stock there is no difference, and besides, Wicksell argued, it is hardly possible for manufacturing to live a life that is isolated from agriculture. On the contrary, 'it must necessarily build on agriculture as its foundation and be limited by the extent of the latter' (Wicksell, 1914: 7). Hence, what goes for agriculture must in one way or another also be true for industry. Cutting the size of the Swedish population in half, would on the other hand ensure that every farmer family would have at least ten hectares at its disposal and 'certainly increase the prosperity of our country to an unimagined extent' (Wicksell, 1914: 8).

Reducing the Swedish labor force would produce a substantial wage increase and reduce the share of capital in the value of production to far more modest dimensions than the contemporary ones (Wicksell, 1923: 310). The empirical evidence was there. It was in the colonies with their far lower population densities that the highest wage rates were found, not in countries that had been cultivated for centuries or millennia.

The frequently adduced counterexample of Ireland after the emigration following the famine years of the 1840s was not valid. In Ireland, wages had fallen to the mere subsistence level during the famine, to the point where no further reduction was possible. They were no longer set by competition but 'by the necessity of not leaving the worker completely without means for his subsistence' (Wicksell, 1923: 311). The situation resembled the one analyzed by Arthur Lewis (1954), where 'a quite substantial reduction of the population must take place before the law of demand and supply could exert its influence so as to increase wages' (Wicksell, 1923: 311). What Wicksell describes is nothing but the surplus labor case of modern development economics.

Diminishing returns in infrastructure

Diminishing returns were also present in the creation of the infrastructure on which economic production was dependent. In an article from 1890 (Wicksell, 1999c), written and published before he wrote the French prize essay, Wicksell criticizes a work by Eb. D'Avis (1889), which dealt with the problem of overproduction, in which the author had expressed his concerns about employing the reduction of output as a remedy, as this would reduce the wage sum of the workers with the same amount. Wicksell points out that this argument fails to include the part accruing to capital. International trade could provide a solution, but the countries of Europe were too much alike in their production structures to offer much scope for intra-European trade. The markets had to be sought overseas.

Wicksell accuses D'Avis of having neglected the growth of the population – his 'main error' (Wicksell, 1999c: 120). The growth of the population called for an increased consumption of foodstuffs, but in the countries of old culture such growth would hardly be possible unless the infrastructure was developed, and that would in turn require 'a corresponding quantity of more or less lengthy costly preparatory work, which, as it provides no immediate yield, can only be made possible by the annual savings of a part of the population' (Wicksell, 1999c: 121). While D'Avis might have been right in stressing that the savings that took place in Europe in 1850–75 were exceptional, he forgot to conclude that in this case the population growth that took place must be considered as exceptional as well, and that it had to be replaced by a stationary population.

According to Wicksell it was precisely in the interplay between population growth and the need for developing infrastructure that the causes of 'overproduction' had to be sought. Once the most important infrastructural works had been finished, diminishing returns to this activity set in. Thus, these works were undertaken to a lesser extent than before. That in the first place led to unemployment. Possibly, the laid-off workers could be channeled into luxury production, as D'Avis had recommended but, if the population continued to grow, sooner or later the number of redundant workers, and hence consumers, would increase and be compensated by nothing. It was from this sequence, and nothing else, Wicksell argues (1999c: 122), that, for example, the unemployment problem of contemporary Germany derived.

The problem could also be approached from the point of view of the savers who are looking for 'capital goods that yield a monetary return' (Wicksell, 1999c: 123). Clearly, if the domestic return is not high enough, capital will emigrate, and Wicksell argues that it may be better that emigrating workers are supported by emigrating capital than that they emigrate alone, but sooner or later conditions in the recipient countries will resemble those in the countries that labor and capital left. The return to capital will then fall and it will be difficult to obtain a savings rate that could help to sustain the investment that is necessary to sustain a growing population. The stationary state will draw nearer.

The same year, 1890, Wicksell (1890c) published an article in Norwegian – his first 'scientific' paper in economics – which linked up with his critique of D'Avis, in which he made population growth part of a theory of the trade cycle. In this theory, upswings and downswings were determined by investment. A bad outlook for new investment would reduce the demand for capital goods, and hence employment. This would reduce, on the one hand, incomes and the demand for goods and services and, on the other hand, make savings lie idle. The immediate result would be both overproduction and a surplus of money. Wicksell argued that in this situation an adaptive mechanism would come into play. Savings would be reduced, and the demand for goods, especially luxuries, would increase in the face of falling prices, as people would refrain from activities that would put a large demand on the future, notably from early marriages and large families. Some, mainly young, people would emigrate in search of employment, and child mortality would increase. 'In this way, the entire population . . . [would] adapt, although reluctantly, and under many kinds of sufferings' (Wicksell, 1890c: 301). A new equilibrium would be established, and from this, consumption and production would increase again.

Technological pessimism

One of the most frequently used arguments when it comes to refuting theories of stagnation and the stationary state is that technological progress will tend to break up the stagnant equilibrium and raise incomes. Wicksell, however, was a technological pessimist. He did not accept the empirical validity of the argument.

In 1903, Wicksell (1903) published a critique of an article by Johan Leffler (1903) (which had actually been directed against Pontus Fahlbeck), in which Leffler contended that the law of diminishing returns 'also in the countries of old cultivation so far only has a *latent* or *potential* character' (Wicksell, 1903: 169). Leffler (1903: 96) explicitly denied that diminishing returns had set in in any European country whatsoever. Wicksell showed that Leffler confused profitability and returns. Agriculture may continue to be profitable long after diminishing returns have set in, if interest and wages are low enough. Wicksell argued that technological progress matters little, for all it does is to shift the diminishing marginal productivity curve upwards, but that diminishing returns would continue to take their toll, but now from a higher level. Again, he concluded that (Wicksell, 1903: 173):

> . . . keeping the law of agricultural productivity in mind, one inevitably has to reach the conclusion that each and every increase of the population in an old, mainly agricultural, society *in itself* is prone to reduce the level of prosperity in general and the conditions of the workers in particular.

To invoke the ability of inventions and the advance of science to raise the standard of living makes no sense, according to Wicksell, as there are few inventions and even fewer that increase prosperity enough to allow population growth to take place without harmful effects. Most of the time they will simply lead to an increase of the size of the population, as they make it easier to find work. Sooner or later some point is therefore reached where all that the invention can do is to sustain a given population. It cannot serve to underpin any increase (Wicksell, 1999a: 97).

Wicksell firmly believed that this stage had already been reached (Overbeek, 1973: 210):

> . . . to argue that this stage has not yet been reached because new inventions are still to come shows a very unclear way of thinking. It can have been entirely exceeded at that particular time. A little boy receives a new pair of shoes every six months, every time receiving a size larger than before. If, however, the shoes were every time one size too small, he would obviously suffer throughout his entire growth

period from tight shoes. And so it is with this case. The population of a century ago had probably exceeded its optimum considerably. The population living in those years would perhaps now be the optimum, and the current population may, for all I know, be the optimum in another 100 years.

In his *Lectures on Political Economy*, Wicksell (1934: 121–2) points to how technological progress in agriculture will in general be beneficial, but insufficient for the workers when the population is simultaneously growing:

> The consequence of an increase in the number of labourers is not only that the new labourers will find it more difficult to earn a livelihood than the old ones, but also that there will be a lowering of wages *all round* owing to their mutual competition; so that the landowners' share of the product will be correspondingly greater. It may be thought that experience often runs counter to this view: wages sometimes remain unchanged, or even rise, despite a considerable increase in population. But the real cause here is that the conditions of production have been materially changed, in consequence of technical or scientific progress, and not least under the influence of capital accumulation, which we have not yet considered. Similarly, entirely new sources of supply may have been discovered. If, under such circumstances, population remained unchanged, the marginal productivity of labour, and consequently wages, would normally rise very considerably. If population increases, however, both will sink to their original level. In other words, technical progress, so far as the labourers are concerned, only protects them against the absolute fall in wages which would otherwise be inevitable, whilst at the same time in [*sic*] increasing, frequently to a high degree, the surplus accruing to the landlord.

Wicksell saw the effects of technological progress as ambiguous from the wage, and hence poverty, point of view.[1] This shows up in at least two of his works. The first is a paper from 1900 (Wicksell, 1958b) on marginal productivity and distribution, in which, among other things, he discusses the impact of technological change on the marginal productivity of different factors. The question is whether the introduction of machines will lead to higher or lower wages.[2] Wicksell (1958b: 102) stressed that:

> . . . an increase in the total product arising from technical innovations in production need not imply an increase in the marginal productivities of all production factors – and certainly not a uniform increase; it

may even happen that the marginal productivity decreases for one factor, while increasing all the more for another. Either the marginal productivity of labour may increase at the expense of that of land, and therefore wages at the expense of rent, or conversely rent may increase at the expense of wages.

As examples of the former sequence, he cites inventions that increase natural resources and that make it possible to use previously neglected power sources or cultivate hitherto unproductive land, as in the case of crop rotation. This, Wicksell states, makes it possible that rents will fall in agriculture and leave the workers with the entire benefit of the increase in production. The opposite case may occur when an invention renders workers redundant without bringing new natural resources into production, as in the case of labor-saving machinery in agriculture (Wicksell, 1958b: 102–3):

> Of course, even here an increase of the product is not impossible (. . . *theoretically*, there must always be such an increase), for, if the same product can be achieved with fewer workers, the remaining workers should be able to produce something, so that the final result is a greater total product; but it seems to be beyond doubt that this result is nevertheless compatible with a decrease, and even a considerable decrease, in the *marginal* productivity of labour.

Wicksell discussed technological progress and wages in his *Lectures* as well. In a celebrated passage (Wicksell, 1934: 164), he pointed to the possibility that labor-saving technological progress may lead to a reduction of wages. For Wicksell, capital was nothing but the 'original production factors,' labor and land, saved and embedded in it for a certain time interval, and the rate of interest was 'the difference between the marginal productivity of saved-up labour and land and of current labour and land' (Wicksell, 1934: 154).

Following Eugen von Böhm-Bawerk, he made a distinction between the 'height' and 'width' of capital. The former concept refers to the length of time for which the various capital goods are invested and an expansion in height is an increase in the proportion of capital goods invested for longer periods at the expense of those invested for shorter periods, i.e. capital deepening. Width, in turn, refers to the proportion of primary factors annually invested in the replacement of capital goods of various maturity dates, and an expansion in width refers to the proportionate increase in all capital goods of different maturity dates, i.e. capital widening (Blaug, 1968: 555–6).

Wicksell pointed out that capital accumulation will generally lead to a wage increase, whereas technological progress may not (Wicksell 1934: 164):

. . . the position is different where, as may easily happen, some *technical invention* renders long-term investment, even without a simultaneous growth of capital, more profitable (absolutely) than previously. The consequence must necessarily be – so long as no further capital is saved – a diminution in the 'horizontal-dimension' and an increase in the 'vertical-dimension,' so that the quantity of capital used in the course of a year will be reduced; an increased quantity of current labour and land will consequently become available for each year's direct production; and, although this need not necessarily cause their marginal productivity and share in the product to be reduced – since the total product has simultaneously been increased by the technical discovery, yet a reduction may clearly result. The capitalist saver is thus, fundamentally, the friend of labour, though the technical inventor is not infrequently its enemy. The great inventions by which industry has from time to time been revolutionized, at first reduced a number of workers to beggary, as experience shows, whilst causing the profits of the capitalists to soar. There is no need to explain away this circumstance by invoking 'economic friction,' and so on, for it is in full accord with a rational and consistent theory. But it is really not capital which should bear the blame; in proportion as accumulation continues, these evils must disappear, interest on capital will fall and wages will rise – unless the labourers on their part simultaneously counteract this result by a large *increase in their numbers.*

Knut Wicksell's pessimistic views of technological progress and his insistence on the severity of diminishing returns led him to an inevitable conclusion: Sweden as well as the rest of Europe was overpopulated. In the next chapter, we will examine his arguments in this respect more closely and discuss his views of overpopulation in Germany and the connection between overpopulation and war. We will finally deal with Wicksell's pessimism with respect to the possibility of using specialization and international trade to overcome the negative effects of population growth.

5 Overpopulation, specialization, and trade

Overpopulation in Sweden

Knut Wicksell was strongly convinced that Sweden was severely overpopulated. The overpopulation concept he used was that of *relative* overpopulation (see below), and he argued that Sweden was a case in point. He had good reasons. Already during the eighteenth century, the Swedish population had begun to grow more rapidly than before. In 1800, the total population was 32 percent larger than fifty years earlier. This trend would continue during the nineteenth century. After 1810, the number of births increased by about 30 percent to the mid-1820s (1806–10 to 1821–5). At the same time the death rate declined, especially among children. Between 1825 and 1840, the size of the group aged fifteen to nineteen years increased by 50 percent, which in turn resulted in mass emigration and colonization of northern Sweden in the 1860s (Hofsten, 1986: 164–75). Between 1858 and 1867, the number of births had increased considerably in Sweden, and the children born during that period had begun to enter the labor market toward the end of the 1870s – a period characterized by severe recession. The average number of births per family was presumably around four. At the same time, the mortality figure had declined, so that the number of surviving children per family had increased (Kock, 1944: 76–7). From 1850 to 1900, the total population increased from less than 3.5 million to over 5.1 (Hofsten and Lundström, 1976: 13).

Karin Kock (1944: 81) summarizes the social situation that prevailed around the time when Wicksell began to take an interest in the population issue:

> . . . a strong natural rate of population growth that was notable especially for the young who were entering the labor market, an out-migration of young people from agriculture to cities and industrial districts as well as abroad, increasing numbers of surviving children per family and a strongly increasing extramarital fertility, a low standard of living

and dismal housing conditions among workers, both in agriculture and industry, late marriages among the educated classes and a severe recession during the late 1870s which reinforced the unsatisfactory state of things.

Wicksell was worried – not least about the interpretation of the situation. In an appendix to his little book on emigration from 1882, he criticized an article published in *Göteborgs Handels- och Sjöfartstidning* on 30 November 1881. The article contended that it was not possible to speak of overpopulation until 'all sources of help' of a country have been employed and the inhabitants are unable to make more efforts. Wicksell considered this approach ridiculous and bluntly stated that if the word overpopulation could not be employed until all conceivable improvements and reforms have been made, it was certainly better not to use the word at all. Instead, he quoted the definition of relative overpopulation in Johan Leffler's (1881: 111) *Grundlinier till nationalekonomiken*. Relative overpopulation is present as soon as the population actually increases faster than the available means of nutrition. Wicksell argued that at least a partial relative overpopulation – among the age groups that accounted for most of the emigration – characterized Sweden in the 1870s (Wicksell, 1882: 99).

Five years later, in 1887, Wicksell published a pamphlet, *Om folkökningen i Sverige* (*On the Population Increase in Sweden*), with the telling subtitle *och de faror den medför för det allmänna välståndet och för sedligheten* (*And the Dangers It Entails for General Welfare and for Morality*) (Wicksell, 1887a). During the preparation of the pamphlet, 'the Malthusian' (*Malthusianaren*), as August Strindberg called him (Gårdlund, 1990: 79), had again caused a public scandal. In 1886 and 1887, Wicksell had spoken on the subject of population on ten occasions during a lecture tour to Swedish cities and Copenhagen (Gårdlund, 1990: 88–9). He had trouble already in Lund, where the police tried to prevent him from finding a venue for a speech on prostitution. 'A more satanic hole than Lund I cannot dream of,' he wrote in a letter dated 5 May 1887 (Hashimoto, 1997: 98), and when he attempted to give talks in Jönköping and Linköping the magistrates of these two cities prohibited the meetings on the pretext that the contents of his lectures were known from other occasions to be 'harmful to discipline and morality.' Wicksell, who in two letters dated 7 and 9 June (Hashimoto, 1997: 106–7) remarked that a 'high point of madness was reached today in Jönköping', and 'Now they are completely devilish' in Linköping, filed a protest to the Swedish Parliamentary Ombudsman and – surprisingly – the Department of Justice took action and convicted both the Mayor of Jönköping and the members of the Magistrate of Linköping for breach of duty and fined them (Gårdlund, 1996: 93).[1]

What was it that the two provincial audiences were not allowed to listen to? Wicksell began by noting that general happiness and satisfaction were not characteristics of Sweden, because important groups in society were 'on the brink of economic disaster' (Wicksell, 1887a: 6), on their way to leave the country. Mortality had declined in virtually all age groups, notably among infants, but regrettably this decline had not been accompanied by any corresponding decline in fertility: The inevitable result was that the growth of the population had accelerated to rates never experienced hitherto. One consequence of this was that wealth was subdivided by inheritance much faster than before and Wicksell considered it to be an open question whether the growth of national wealth had proceeded fast enough to outweigh this effect.

As a result, farmers' children were forced to leave the countryside and attempt to eke out a living in urban areas, where most likely they would find their capital insufficient, go bankrupt and be proletarianized. Wicksell argued that the consequences of this process would have shown up long ago were it not for the fact that Sweden, especially during the last three decades, had borrowed abroad. He estimated the Swedish foreign debt to around 600 million kronor, with yearly interest and amortization payments in the order of 30 million, had Sweden bothered to honor its commitments. Wicksell doubted whether, as alleged, Sweden's foreign debt was harmless, as the money borrowed had been invested productively. At least it had to be proved that the loans had increased productivity enough to cover both increased consumption and payments on the debt. Wicksell was certain that the hangover from the borrowing feast would come. When the debt finally had to be repaid, it would cause a reduction of consumption and welfare that would be larger than the corresponding increase made possible by the loans. He was utterly pessimistic (Wicksell, 1887a: 22):

> The state of our country ... will then appear almost like that of unfortunate Ireland, whose cereals, pork and linen cloths every year are exported as tribute to some landowners residing outside the country and their entourage, while large parts of the population are said to live in a state of almost perennial famine.

Wicksell contended that fertility had to be reduced by at least one-third in order to arrive at the equilibrium between birth and death rates. This was 'the least that has to be done if we are to be in the position where we are able to face the economic future of our country with reasonable confidence' (Wicksell, 1887a: 25).

Overpopulation and war

In Wicksell's view, the growth of the population was intimately connected with the risk of war. In his 1880 lectures he emphasized two checks of population growth: war and emigration. That he took the war issue seriously was made clear in the French prize essay. There he contended that arguments in favor of high population growth that conceived of national glory in terms of population size are only superficial. Besides an excessive population in a country will always entail the risk of war. Europe was 'au grand complet' (Wicksell, 1979: 149), and this, in turn, made it necessary to ensure that everywhere the economies of neighboring countries would flourish. Wicksell explicitly points to Germany, arguing that despite of all its economic progress that country has not managed to feed its population. 'What will be the end? Some war?' (Wicksell, 1891: 297). Prophetic words, indeed.

In 1914, the war was a fact, and two years later Wicksell published an article in the Italian journal *Scientia*, in which he stressed population growth as a cause of war (Wicksell, 1916b). Wicksell's mood was optimistic, however. His starting point was a number of articles published by the well-known Danish literary historian and critic Georg Brandes, who mocked those who thought that the Great War would be the war that would end all wars. Brandes argued that the same argument had been advanced after the Franco-Prussian War in 1870–1, and that it assumed no less than a radical change in human nature.

Wicksell found Brandes' view too pessimistic and argued that during the period that had elapsed between the two wars a major change had taken place, which would diminish the risk of future wars. That change was '*the pronounced reduction of the number of births* that is taking place in virtually all the civilized countries on earth' (Wicksell, 1916b: 457). This would not simply lead to a slower growth of the population but also, in the longer run, to a reduction of its size. It was clear for Wicksell that whatever the immediate causes of the World War may have been, they would not have sufficed to trigger the disaster had it not been for the fact that real wages had been falling despite rapid technical progress. The cause was the too rapid growth of the population in almost all of the powers at war. The reduced birth rates had been accompanied by reduced death rates, and population growth had remained high. However, as death rates had fallen to such a low level that Wicksell did not believe that they could fall much further, continued reduction of the birth rates would sooner or later make for lower population sizes as well. Using German statistical evidence that tends to confirm his views, Wicksell extrapolates the trends that he is discerning to the rest of Europe as well and concludes on a happy note (Wicksell, 1916b:

466): 'A pacific coexistence and collaboration of peoples that all possess, within their own borders, a space that is large enough for their activities is no longer a utopia.'

Wicksell continued with the war subject even after World War I. He included an economic analysis of the war in the topics for lectures to be given during a summer course at Uppsala University in 1919 (Wicksell, 1978). The last part of his lecture was devoted to overpopulation as a cause of the war. Wicksell stated bluntly that it is the strife over territory that 'in all periods has constituted the foremost if not the only reason for war,' and behind the desire for expansion was always the growth of the population (Wicksell, 1978: 246). Religious wars, wars of independence and civil wars alike were ultimately driven by the lack of space to feed the population. Wars and population growth tended to form a vicious circle (Wicksell, 1978: 247):

> Throughout history increases in population and wars condition each other in an eternal *circulus vitiosus*. For if on the one hand overcrowding creates the necessity and longing for a war, a numerous population on the other hand is a prerequisite for victory. Therefore steps to check the increase of population in a peaceful way by decreasing birth-rates will always encounter resistance among the ruling and military classes; and at the end of the war, be it won or lost, nothing is generally considered more important than to encourage a strong increase in the population in order to 'fill the cadres' again.

Germany was an obvious example for Wicksell, who pointed out that the 'feverish industrial development' of the pre-war period, when the production of coal doubled, that of lignite quadrupled and that of pig-iron tripled during a twenty-year period, while at the same time the country became severely overpopulated, could not have continued. Even though Germany had lost the war, the concomitant loss of population would ease the situation 'to a considerable extent' before 'the ruling circles' would again start to promote population growth (Wicksell, 1978: 247).

Wicksell went even further, arguing that if the world population would continue to grow on the same scale as during the nineteenth century, 'all hopes for a world peace would be in vain' (Wicksell, 1978: 247–8). However, if war and population growth form a vicious circle, there is of course no reason why peace and population control should not constitute a virtuous one. Wicksell saw it as a hopeful sign that in 'well-nigh all civilized countries' the birth control movement was growing stronger, not least in Germany, and he even contended, with an argument that he appears to have borrowed from his friend Hjalmar Öhrvall, that it was the realization that the German population would decline that made the military strike precisely in 1914 (Wicksell, 1978: 248).

Seven years later, in one of his last manuscripts (based on a lecture) before his death (Wicksell, 1926b), Wicksell came back to the connection between overpopulation and war, bringing up a second kind of two-way relationship between them. He began by noting that among all the remedies for overpopulation war has at all times been without competition the most popular one and in addition 'in olden days' the most efficient one (Wicksell, 1926b: 262). The two-way relationship, however, had been broken in his own time (Wicksell, 1926b: 264):

> ... while one side of the causal relationship: war as a remedy for overpopulation in our time has all but disappeared, or even been converted into its opposite, unfortunately the other side still exists: overpopulation as a cause of war. In the days of mercenary armies this circumstance was obvious. A sergeant who is recruiting, says Malthus, prays to heaven for crop failure and unemployment, i.e. for an abundance of people. This was what made the youths rally around the flags, like it had previously driven them to Viking raids or crusades. For the ruler the filling of the cadres thus turned into a barometer of an impending overpopulation and at the same time a means of enforcing his will that he did not hesitate to make use of, so much more since maintenance always cost money. There was always a reason for war in some direction.
>
> In our days universal military service prevails, the cadres are always full, the war machine, so to speak, always has the steam up.

Wicksell, who got engaged in most social and economic issues of his day, could not refrain from getting involved in the German reparation problem either (Wicksell, 1921a; 1921b; 1922; 1923). This would later give rise to the celebrated theoretical debate carried out between Maynard Keynes (1929) and Bertil Ohlin (1929) on the transfer problem (see Mundell, 2002, for an account of their debate). Wicksell, however, had a different angle. He turned the reparation problem into yet another aspect of the population question. Wicksell refuted those who argued that it would be impossible to mobilize enough of the accumulated German savings to defray the payments, including Keynes, who wrote *The Economic Consequences of the Peace* in 1919 (Keynes, 1919), as the savings would be needed to provide the growing German population with housing, tools, and household capital goods. If so, conceded Wicksell, it might be impossible to handle the reparation, but if the size of the German population could be brought down, this argument would fall. The accumulated savings could then be freed for reparation purposes, and in addition, mobilizing additional saving would be easier in families with fewer children. Fortunately, he observed, German fertility was on its way down.

The Economic Consequences of the Peace appeared in Swedish translation in 1920 (Keynes, 1920), and in August 1921 Keynes published an article in the Swedish newspaper *Dagens Nyheter* (Keynes, 1921a), commenting on the further elaboration of the positions of the victors vis-à-vis Germany (see Skidelsky, 1992: chapter 2). In this article, Keynes argued that although the new proposal, put forward in May 1921, was better than the one contained in the Treaty of Versailles, it would serve only to give the Germans a little breathing space until 1922. His basic argument remained the same as in *The Economic Consequences of the Peace*: payment of the amounts demanded by the victors would serve to depress the standard of living of the German population to an unacceptably low level.

Nine days after the appearance of Keynes' article, Wicksell published a comment on it in *Dagens Nyheter* (Wicksell, 1921b), where he reiterated the argument that the observed reduction in German fertility would make fulfillment of the payment obligations possible and accused Keynes of having made 'a fundamental mistake' in his calculation by not taking this into account. Wicksell requested that a translation be forwarded to Keynes. The reply he received, via the newspaper, was a nasty one (Hashimoto, forthcoming, Letter 165):

> Many thanks for sending me the translation of Professor Wicksell's article. He raises a highly interesting point, and one which I should like to deal with. But I confess that if he intends his arguments to be applicable, not merely hypothetically, but to the real conditions of to-day, what he says strikes me as academic in the worst sense of the word. I stated clearly in my articles[2] that I was dealing only with the near future; and if he thinks that the kind of considerations he is raising affect that, I am sure that he is gravely mistaken.

Wicksell, however, did not give up. In October 1921, he wrote a letter to Keynes, where again he exposed his views on the subject, only to receive another acid response (Hashimoto, forthcoming, Letter 164):

> I entirely agree that when one is dealing with the wider subject it is necessary to pay attention to your argument. I agree that an important part of Germany's pre-war savings were required to look after the growing population and that economy in his respect would increase the surplus available for other purposes to a certain extent. But I believe I could produce a hundred reasons (perhaps you will excuse me from

entering into detail, as my correspondence is now overwhelming) for thinking that in practice this factor cannot be quantitatively important. Let me remind you in particular that additional house room is mainly required, not for new-born babies, but for young couples growing up and marrying. There is therefore a very material time-lag between a decrease in the birth rate and a decrease in the number of couples growing up and marrying.

Specialization and trade: a non-solution

Wicksell argued that the existence of an industrial sector was a sign of progress in a country beyond the satisfaction of the mere basic needs, and the as yet not finished colonization of overseas territories had led to a division of labor that allowed Europe to subsist on grain and other foodstuffs from overseas and from Eastern Europe (Wicksell, 1999d: 148):

> It is for this reason that, over the past century, these old countries have been able to manifest population growth far in excess of what would have been possible purely on the basis of the development of western Europe's own agriculture, no matter how splendid the progress has in fact been in the domain of agricultural technology [...] In other words, the industry of the western European countries has grown far beyond the proportions to which it would have been confined if it had still constituted merely a superstructure on domestic agriculture; it largely leads an independent life, based on the *world-wide* exchange of industrial items for agricultural products . . .

This development, however, had its own inherent dangers. Repeating the argument from the 1891 prize essay, only more forcefully than twenty years before, Wicksell in 1910 argued that the extensive trade of industrial goods for food was likely to be nothing but a temporary episode in economic history. In the first place, the colonial countries would themselves be running into diminishing returns to labor in agriculture and hence put more of their labor force into industry, and they would become the main consumers of their agricultural produce (Wicksell, 1999d: 148–9):

> It is revealing in this regard that the United States, which until recently was Europe's foremost granary and the principal centre of the dreaded 'trans-oceanic competition' in the corn market, has now almost reached stagnation in its production of cereals, particularly of *wheat*, while Canada and still more so Argentina are making rapid advances, as are the areas in the south and east of Russia that have similarly only

been colonized in recent times. When it comes to the export of *maize*, too, Argentina is not so far behind the United States these days, and the latter country also shows a significant surplus of *imports* of sugar, hides, wool, silk and rubber; only when it comes to *cotton* does it still retain its leading position among agricultural export countries.

This development was sped up by the introduction of tariffs on manufactures, which in turn made it more difficult for the western European countries to dispose of their industrial surplus and hence also to cover their food needs via imports. The direct cause of protectionism was the growth of the population. In *Finanzteoretische Untersuchungen*, Wicksell (1896b: 64) points out that 'The urge to protect domestic industries will make itself felt as soon as the country has a population large enough to lead to the emergence of rent on a significant scale, with the wage level still appreciably larger than in the old countries.' The introduction of the tariff would serve to increase wages at the expense of rent.

The second danger that Wicksell saw with specialization and trade was that the stocks of mineral raw materials and fossil fuels would be exhausted in the sense that the cost of employing them would increase rapidly, faster than what might be compensated for by material-saving technological progress. Again, Wicksell ended his discussion on a profoundly pessimistic note (Wicksell, 1999d: 149):

> What I here considered important to stress was merely a fact that is basically self-evident, but is so often overlooked, namely, that even though the modern development or rather revolutionizing of European industry has in fact extended over a period of several generations, it is necessarily purely temporary by nature; a fact that moreover, as I have said, is self-evident on account of the absurd consequences that arise when one imagines it continuing on the same scale even for just a few more centuries into the future.

In the specific case of Sweden, the picture did not look too good either. The iron ore deposits would last for quite some time, even at the contemporary rate of depletion the forests provided a renewable raw material, and the Swedish water power resources could continue to be developed. Although production for the domestic market was limited by the extent of this development, an extent in the end conditioned by the country's agricultural development, production for export was a different matter. On the other hand, an examination of the available statistics led Wicksell to conclude that it was only in the case of wood and pulp products that Sweden had a real export surplus, but maintaining that surplus on the same scale as hitherto would require cutting at a rate by far exceeding that of the growth of the Swedish forests. This in turn called for processing, but for processed wood products the situation was complicated by tariffs abroad. Wicksell did not see any possibilities of finding any substitutes for wood and pulp exports in the short run and was afraid that iron production would experience a contraction as well (Wicksell, 1999d: 154):

> If, therefore, an answer is required to the question of whether our industry is likely in the immediate future to absorb the surplus population that will otherwise have to seek its way by emigrating, then on the basis of the facts *now* available this answer can hardly be anything but *negative*.

A third obstacle to continued international trade was found on the demand side in the New World. In his booklet on population, Wicksell (1979: 148) quoted figures on the discrepancy between population growth and food production in Europe, which indicated that at the end of the twentieth century the demand for food imports in Western Europe would amount to three times the figure for 1890. He, however, doubted that this figure would suffice, as in the extreme case when agricultural production in Western Europe would remain stationary, although the population would treble its size, the correct figure would be eight to ten times as high as the 1890 one. To satisfy this demand via imports would be impossible, as at the same time the population of the food-exporting countries would increase, consume the formerly available food surplus and, in addition, cease to demand Western European manufactures (Wicksell, 1979: 148):

> But those countries which are now the granaries of Europe – the United States, Russia, the East Indies, Australia, Argentina and Canada – do not themselves have stationary populations. They are growing, and even at a greater speed than Western Europe itself. Although the initial phase of colonization of a previously uninhabited country leads to an ever-increasing surplus of grain and meat, the condition will of course soon become the reverse. It is therefore only a matter of time, probably only a few decades, until these countries, particularly the last three, will themselves consume the totality of their present food surpluses and at the same time, as the result of heir own industrial growth, essentially cease to be consumers of Western European manufactures.

In 1926, Wicksell noted that the golden age of north–south factor proportions based trade had come to an end. In fact, he had been expecting it, as the international exchange of manufactured products for food staples constituted a disturbing ingredient in his view of long-run economic development, a view that rested heavily on diminishing returns to a too rapidly growing population (see Uhr, 1962: 328–9). Wicksell summarized what he considered to be the exceptional episode of the nineteenth century (Wicksell, 1926b: 265):

> The curious episode in world history that was constituted by the gigantic population growth of the nineteenth century may now be regarded as finished. It rested on two main factors: the utilization of the transoceanic continents for world communications, for the European immigration and indirectly for the European industry, as well as the utilization of the subterranean bodies: the layers of coal as a source of power and heating for this industry and for the population in general. It is in the nature of the matter that the continuous extensive development on a marvelous, never previously attained, scale that was hereby made possible cannot continue.

Wicksell (1925: 10) pointed to the 'artificial economic life' of Western Europe, with its concentration on manufactures and its imports of food and raw materials from overseas and from Russia. What would later, by Folke Hilgerdt (League of Nations, 1945), be termed the regions of recent settlement – the United States, Canada, Argentina, Uruguay, and Australia – the regions that supplied food to Europe, saw their populations grow, and in the end they would reach population densities that would not allow them to produce an exportable surplus any more. Diminishing returns in agriculture would take their toll. Europe itself would have to produce the primary products it needed and that would not be possible unless the density of its population was reduced.

6 Emigration
A solution of the past

Toward the end of 1881, Knut Wicksell gave a lecture in Stockholm (twice) and Uppsala on the importance and causes of emigration, which he also published the following year (Wicksell, 1882).[1] His point of departure was that at least 100,000 Swedes had left the country during 1880 and 1881 (the vast majority for the United States), a figure that he considered large for a country of 4.5 million inhabitants. In Sweden, large-scale emigration had begun in the 1860s (Hofsten and Lundström, 1976: 68), with a peak in 1868–9, when 66,000 people departed after fatal harvests. A second wave began in 1879 and continued up until 1893. During this period, more than 565,000 people – the equivalent of 37 percent of all of the emigrants between 1851 and 1930 – left Sweden. The peak years were 1882 (50,000), 1887 (51,000) and 1888 (another 50,000), about eleven per thousand of the total population each year.

Views were split on whether emigration was good or bad for Sweden, and Wicksell set out to examine the actual effects. Whether the emigrant succeeds or not, he writes, has no impact on the Swedish economy, unless we take income remittances into account, but such remittances he considers in general to be 'of a temporary and passing nature' (Wicksell, 1882: 13). The main effects have to be sought elsewhere, and Wicksell argued that emigration leads to a 'double' loss. In the first place, capital is required both for the voyage and for the first few months in the foreign country. Still, Wicksell considered this effect to be less important. Emigrants, he argued, usually finance their trip by sales of their assets, but in the Swedish case most of them were 'workers and servants' (Wicksell, 1882: 15), i.e. poor people with little to sell. Frequently, they were financed by relatives already in the new country or by loans that they later had to repay. Thus, Wicksell concluded, in quantitative terms, there was not too much to argue about.

A human capital perspective

Far more important, quantitatively speaking, is the loss of *human* capital – of labor – and this will in turn have consequences in the labor market (Wicksell, 1882: 19):

> The most certain and most immediate consequence of emigration is that it reduces the competition among the workers and hence increases wages or, if the latter are already on the decrease, counteracts their further reduction. Moreover, even though the workers who remain behind thus get an occasion to increase their consumption, the reduction of the number of consumers should still make the price of all such commodities that are not completely dependent on the position of prices in the foreign market cheaper.

This, from the distributional point of view, would be positive (Wicksell, 1882: 19):

> Both these circumstances concretely speaking constitute a decided advantage for the majority of the population, and, even though their impact on those classes in society who to a larger or smaller extent live by the work of others is not as favorable (unless the expenditure on relief for the poor is reduced), in the face of a non-partial judgment the advantages in this respect must be considered to outweigh the disadvantages by far.

Wicksell came back to wages as a class issue in a pamphlet on sexual questions, published in 1890, when he attacked a professor of medicine from Lund, Seved Ribbing, for his views on sexuality and population (Wicksell, 1890a). Ribbing (1889) had contended that the wealthy classes in Sweden were against early marriages and numerous children among the working classes, because that would increase expenditure on poverty relief. Wicksell (1890a: 97) gave Ribbing a formidable whipping:

> For had wages already sunk to the minimum that, according to the, however, rather differing yardstick of each separate country and point in time, is considered necessary for the sustenance of a family, a further increase of the numbers of the working classes cannot lead to any lowering of this minimum but only to increased poverty relief taxes. Among our dispossessed agricultural workers this limit has seldom been reached in practice. But as long as it has not been reached to the full extent, it is undeniably in the interest of the propertied classes

that 'a supply of cheap labor,' as they so prettily put it, should not be lacking. That this circumstance in turn has dictated the reception that the Malthusian and especially neo-Malthusian doctrines have met with from the upper classes you have to be virtually naïve to doubt.

In his lecture on the economic effects of the Great War, Wicksell came back to 'the social question.' A reduction of the size of the working class would make wages rise, make it easier to push for the eight-hour working day and make it necessary to pursue a more equitable distribution of property, i.e. prerequisites would be 'created for a successful settlement of the social question' (Wicksell, 1978: 248).

Wicksell was not prepared to endorse the idea that labor migration is an unmitigated blessing. There was still another 'debit' item: the cost of education that accrues to the home country and which does not correspond to any contribution to production by the emigrants. This was the most important aspect for Wicksell (1882: 23):

> If ... it turns out that the country has not been able to educate this labor which it does not need without high, perhaps enormous, costs, it appears to be hence that the economic point of gravity of the question moves, and it matters little or nothing that the emigration at the time when it is produced by the circumstances may constitute a true relief for the country.

To this decidedly long-run view, which assumes that at some point the migrants can be employed at home, Wicksell added an explicit human capital perspective (Wicksell, 1882: 24):

> The education and care that is thus bestowed upon the adolescent generation should be regarded as an advance in terms of capital that it must, in its turn, repay some time, mainly by caring for a subsequent generation. For each individual that leaves the realm (or is carried off by death) before he has had the time to repay his share in this debt a loss is obviously inflicted on the country through the capital invested in him but not repaid.

Wicksell estimated the human capital lost through emigration during 1880 and 1881 to be in the order of 70 million kronor (Wicksell, 1882: 24–9). Should it, on the other hand, turn out to be impossible to employ the emigrants at home, their emigration should be regarded simply as a way of writing off a loss that has already been incurred by their home country. Then the emigrants from the economic point of view constitute a worthless asset, whose nominal book value can never be realized.

The fate of the emigrants

Wicksell also devoted some space to the fate of the emigrants abroad. He complained that the information with respect to the fates of Swedish emigrants to the United States was both meager and contradictory. He concluded, however, that they should be more exposed to changes in the level of economic activity than native Americans, and that often what they had to do was to go west and settle on homesteads on the very land frontier where, even during good years, the price obtained barely sufficed to cover the transportation costs. Should the price fall, however, the immigrant would be in trouble. For example, at the end of 1873 the American economy went into a recession, and an article published in the Swedish periodical *Samtiden* in 1874, which dealt with the conditions that the emigrants met, gave rise to the following reflections (Wicksell, 1882: 35–6):

> The colors in which the fate of the unfortunate emigrant are . . . painted are so utterly dark that one must ask oneself whether for the fortunately not particularly important numbers of emigrants who that year left our country to cross the Atlantic it would not have been better that they had perished on the open sea instead of landing on a coast where only a rapid destruction awaited them. For it should be clear from what has already been said about the capital wealth accompanying the emigrants that if it is difficult for many to depart for America, for more than one, returning will be a sheer impossibility. But whatever the fate of a man, and even more of a woman, must be under such circumstances, it is not necessary to speak of it, since my task is not to strike the cords of sentimentality, unless they vibrate by themselves at the mere mention of such sad circumstances.

Worse than the emigration to the United States was the quantitatively smaller emigration of servants from southern Sweden to northern Germany and Denmark. Wicksell (1882: 38–9) was more than indignant:

> Public authorities and private persons have often and with emphasis argued against this emigration which through its consequences undeniably comes close to being a national scandal, but in the home districts of those who depart it is not viewed, so I have been told, with unfavorable eyes, since the community in this way is rid of some of its worst elements. For it is not, as is easily understood, the sons and daughters of wealthy landowners who are lured into a foreign country in order to serve there for a wage that has little or anything in common with what is offered at home, but it is generally the worst refuse of the parishes, children who have grown up in the worst of homes and from

whom nothing else can be expected than following in the footsteps of their fathers and mothers; and people are happy to be rid of them for the time being. Usually, however, they come back in a few years, and at that point the last confusion becomes worse than the first one. The young men during their ambulant way of life most of the time have been imbibed with raw and destructive habits, and as far as the young women are concerned, in an official document about this matter it is stated that they 'usually return home exploited and disgraced.' In recent years it has happened several times that the return journey has been made as a prisoner and under the most heartbreaking circumstances.

Wicksell painted the life cycle of the young woman coming from the most destitute of family backgrounds, who does anything to get away and, once at her new destination, has to struggle with a foreign language, but who will at long last learn at least what '*hübsches Mädchen*' means and whose fate, from the time when she chooses to take the compliment seriously, is sealed. She gives birth as a single mother and in the end is forced to make the trip home as a prisoner. The rest of the story, Wicksell (1882: 42) argued, is not terribly interesting: 'how she with her child or her children is accommodated in the poorhouse, a target for the mockery of her sisters in misfortune . . .' After this tirade, followed by a brief discussion of how Swedes become thieves in Denmark, he was ready for his conclusion (Wicksell, 1882: 44):

> Our final judgment on emigration can hence not be unconditionally positive. It may be the case that during times of economic distress and unemployment it can constitute a valuable, but generally insufficient, means for improving the position. Thus it would be highly unwise to attempt to hamper or reduce the emigration by means of force, as was the practice in ancient times and as is still sometimes suggested. On the other hand, this movement, especially if regarded as a recurrent phenomenon, possesses so many doubtful sides that it would doubtlessly be really beneficial for our country if in the future it could be forestalled or at least reduced by natural means that do not include force.

The obvious cause

However, these means cannot be designed unless we are equipped with proper knowledge of what causes emigration. Wicksell was not in the slightest doubt. Alleged causes like religious intolerance could explain only 'the tens and the hundreds' in the numbers of emigrants (Wicksell, 1882: 47). He also rejected that it should be the conditions in the United States that served as a magnet, as the emigration from Sweden received a hitherto unknown boost after the years of severe Swedish harvest failure at the end of the 1860s. Before 1868, emigration from Sweden had been insignificant, caused mainly by such factors as religious oppression and limitations on the freedom of speech, on average less than one-half per thousand of the population. The fatal year 1868, when the harvest failed, however, sent a shock wave through the country, and the following year the figure soared to nine per thousand. This emigration boom was to last for six years, before it began to taper off during the relatively good years of 1872–3, only to pick up again after the turn for worse in 1878, and a new maximum was reached 1880–2, ten per thousand, in the main young people who had difficulties getting a job (Kock, 1944: 80–1).

It was thus quite obvious that there was a connection between the economic situation in Sweden and the rate of emigration. The cause of emigration, Wicksell (1882: 53) argued, must be sought in the excessive growth of the population. He calculated that the number of inhabitants between twenty-one and thirty years of age in Sweden would have been 60,000–70,000 higher in 1881, were it not for the emigration. Compared with 1871, that figure would represent an increase in 25 percent – of people in the age when marriage and family formation normally took place (Wicksell, 1882: 55).

It was clear for Wicksell that this was a potentially Malthusian situation, as he could not conceive of any possibility that the growth of agriculture and industry would have been fast enough to accommodate five new families instead of four. He did not deny that both agriculture and manufacturing had taken great strides forward, but not enough to accommodate those who emigrated and their would-be families. The land could not be subdivided indefinitely, so the agricultural sector would have to shed labor and these workers would be 'compressed' within the narrower limits of industry and commerce – sectors that were both far smaller than agriculture: a veritable inundation. Thus, there was only one possible conclusion (Wicksell, 1882: 61):

> If we want to reduce the inconveniences of population growth there is no better means for this than to reduce the growth of the population itself; if in the future we want to forestall emigration or at least reduce it to less frightening proportions we must stop breeding emigrants.

Changing viewpoints

In 1887, Wicksell had sharpened his attitude toward emigration. He rejected emigration, as 'the worst conceivable means.' To breed 'human cattle for export free of charge' was degrading and, besides, in the near future this escape valve would be closed or at least more difficult to use than in the past (Wicksell, 1887a: 26). The agricultural frontier extending from north to south in the United States was more or less closed, having reached the Rocky Mountains, leaving 'only pockets and backlands' (Wicksell, 1887a: 27) to be filled. If, in addition, as it seemed, emigration to Canada, Brazil, Australia, and Africa was unsuccessful, the livelihood of the population 'that had been allowed to grow without any clear view of whether the probable development of the means of subsistence of the country would make such an increase advisable' (Wicksell, 1887a: 28) would have to be sought in Sweden itself.

Wicksell was more favorably disposed toward emigration of women than toward emigration of men. This disposition shows up in an unpublished lecture delivered on 11 February 1896 (Wicksell, 1896b). The reason was simple. During the course of emigration more men than women had left in search of a future outside Sweden. Accordingly, Wicksell recommended young women that they should emigrate, preferably to the colonies where there was an acute deficit of females.

Wicksell came back to the emigration issue in more positive terms in 1909 (Wicksell, 1999d), when he was called upon by the Emigration Inquiry to make a statement. This was published the following year as part of an appendix to the main volume. He began by recalling his 1881 lecture, reiterating that he still held the same ideas. Not least was he skeptical to the movement hostile against emigration that had served as a trigger of the Emigration Inquiry. Only if the causes were of a temporary nature would such hostility be warranted; were they of a more permanent nature it would be a mistake to prevent emigration from taking place.

Wicksell proceeded to examine the home ownership movement in Sweden. The idea was to provide couples who wanted to purchase their own home with loans. Wicksell criticizes the idea because of the small sums involved, especially in the case of farms, arguing that they would only serve to produce a new proletariat. To create new farms would make no sense, as in Sweden, 'a country of old cultivation' (Wicksell, 1999d: 141), the land most suitable for farming in the long run had already been put under cultivation (Wicksell, 1999d: 141–2):

> The hackneyed cliché in the newspapers about Norrland as our America, our 'land of future,' etc., ought therefore to be abandoned. In fact, as is well known, Norrland currently exhibits a considerable surplus of out-migration, not just to foreign countries but now apparently also to the other parts of our country. It therefore seems to be far from capable even of supporting its own 'natural' population increase, its colossally high surplus of births – the only respect in which Norrland continues to exhibit any resemblance to a colony.

Wicksell, always a pessimist in this matter, argued that it was far from certain that technological progress would solve the productivity problems of agriculture, as some innovations would simply not be profitable. Again he made the distinction between extensive and intensive agriculture and pointed to the land as the limiting factor in terms of production per worker, arguing that farm size was often far too small in Sweden. The only possible conclusion was that no obstacles should be put in the way of migration (Wicksell, 1999d: 146):

> To the extent . . . that the surplus of our agricultural population is unable to find employment within industry, it seems to me that we ought not to combat but to aid and support the endeavours of that population to find 'homes of their own' in those parts of the world where such homes can still be acquired on reasonable terms. [. . .] But as far as I know, not even in years of famine has the Swedish state ever contributed as much as an *öre* to this kind of home ownership movement, or devoted a single thought to it – other than to put short-sighted barriers in its way.

After having examined the situation in both agriculture and industry, Wicksell hastened to stress that the *real* emigration issue is connected with the growth of the population. To argue that the size of the population should be expanded was simply foolish (Wicksell, 1999d: 155):

> . . . those who make rapid population growth their ideal, without scrutinizing the consequences, commit an act of folly; they 'pray badly.' for in reality they may be praying for typhus and cholera, rickets and tuberculosis, poverty, ignorance and prostitution, prisons and hospitals filled beyond capacity, social discontent and acts of violence by left-wing extremists . . .

Wicksell stressed that the issue was not the maximum possible population but its optimum size, 'the number that in the given conditions is best suited to the available natural resources and is therefore most compatible with the achievement of material well-being, which is after all the necessary basis for all other culture' (Wicksell, 1999d: 157). He concluded that in the case of Sweden the optimum figure was far below the actual one. Here emigration could be of help. In fact, it might be impossible to reduce the population to the extent needed without resorting to 'considerably augmented' emigration (Wicksell, 1999d: 160). Of course, finding a place to go to could be difficult, and Wicksell came up with the not too realistic proposal that Siberia could provide an outlet (Wicksell, 1999d: 161):

One receives the impression from books and travellers' accounts that by reason of their natural conditions, the forested tracts of southern Siberia would be well-suited to Scandinavian immigrants, better even than to Russian peasants who have grown up on the plains, but who are now almost alone in populating these tremendous expanses on a large scale. The question must at least be raised – and ought also to be investigated more loosely – whether *colonization*, preferably joint colonization by the Scandinavian countries and Finland (which in my opinion are all in about equally great need of emigration), might not be feasible in these parts, with the permission of the Russian authorities. To be sure, in itself the idea of placing oneself under the rule of the Tsar cannot possibly be very tempting at the present time. But of course it is likely that in time, internal conditions in Russia, too, will improve, and reportedly, among the people of Siberia in particular, a much freer spirit prevails than in Russia proper – there the Russian saying that 'the Tsar is remote' applies in an even higher degree and in a *better* sense.[2]

Still, Wicksell argued, emigration can never be anything more than a palliative, as when time goes by the empty and half-empty lands will be filled with people and then the only solution that remains is to reduce the number of births.[3] There is no such thing as a 'normal' rate of population growth. Every increase is more or less anomalous. Therefore, Wicksell recommended that the population question 'should be regarded and dealt with as the great national concern it actually is' (Wicksell, 1999d: 163). He spoke in no uncertain terms (Wicksell, 1999d: 164):

> ... the normal thing, and in the long run the only possible thing in our country as in all countries, is a population that is stationary in numerical terms, and what is more, such a population is the necessary condition for a land *not* remaining stationary or even going backwards in all other respects than the purely numerical. This is as certain and as self-evident as that two times two is four; and any calculation of the future, any economic policy, that does not build on this simple fact as its foundation, belongs to realm of fantasies and dreams, not the real world.

In 1910, Wicksell had sharpened his tone. Instead of recommending a moderate increase of the population, as in 1880, he advocated zero growth, at a lower absolute level: the optimum level.

7 The optimum population

Joseph Spengler (1983: 5) has summarized the implications of Wicksell's insistence on diminishing returns:

> One may say in conclusion that Wicksell's emphasis upon the role of diminishing returns and the resulting limitations to the augmentability of the total output in a given country made evident the costs of population growth beyond certain limits. This discovery in turn drew attention to the fact that population growth beyond a certain point made for a decline in the realizable level of average output, that is, at a point that marked a country's optimum size of population, excess of which prevented maximization of average output in such countries. This conception, a derivative of Malthusian concern, won even wider support in the late nineteenth and the twentieth century, due in some part to Wicksell's contributions.

Wicksell himself was quite adamant. On one of the last pages in *Value, Capital and Rent* he suggested attaining the optimal population as the only alternative to fixing wages at the subsistence level (Wicksell, 1954: 166):

> ... so far as I know, the question has never been raised in economic writings, what size of the population is economically most profitable when the amount of capital, size of the area of the land, etc., are given. If, therefore, these problems are to be solved according to the principle of the greatest utility, it is obviously a serious drawback that there is not even common agreement *in what direction* economic advantage or disadvantage in fact lies. If, on the other hand, we assume that changes of population are not regulated according to the principle of what is economically most advantageous (in the widest sense of the word), but are regulated now and for ever merely by blind natural instincts, then at least we are on firm ground. In that case, however, we should have no

alternative but to accept Ricardo's doctrine of the natural wage – that is to say, the smallest possible wage – as a fact beyond dispute.

Wicksell was modest about his contribution to the study of population, but not to the point of considering it unimportant. In a little article from 1910 on the concept of optimum population (Overbeek, 1973: 208) he claimed that the issue was completely under-researched:

> . . . Since it is of a strictly scientific character it is probable that people will ask me what the experts have to say about the guidelines leading to a decision whether the existing population of a country is as large as it should be, too small, or too large. Unfortunately, however, one hears not a word, not a single word, from the experts about this. They are mute on this issue. One can peruse the entire economic literature from now until next Christmas without finding this salient point even mentioned by economists.

On the occasion of Wicksell's sixtieth birthday, the newspaper *Aftontidningen* commissioned a number of well-known Swedes to pay their homage. One of these was Gustaf Steffen, professor of economics and sociology in Gothenburg, who when he came to the population issue thought Wicksell's contributions to be less successful. Wicksell reacted immediately, drafting a letter to the editor (which was, however, never sent off), where he set out to describe his contribution – in modest words (Wicksell, 1911):

> My contribution to the theory of population actually consists in that I have emphasized more forcefully than other economists the fundamentally self-evident proposition that on each technical level there must be an *optimum* population density in each individual country. In addition, stating my reasons, I have professed the opinion that this optimum at present, in our own as well as in other countries, has been *exceeded considerably*, so that the road to national wealth at the present time would lie, not in a further increase, but in a radical *reduction of the size of the population*, continued during several decades.

The two population questions

The optimum population concept constitutes the most important part of Wicksell's first chapter of the first Swedish edition of *Lectures in Political Economy* (Wicksell, 1901). He excluded the chapter from later editions and instead published it as a separate booklet (Wicksell, 1926a; 1979). After covering such issues as the age distribution of the population, its composition by sex and marital status, mortality, fertility, the natural rate of population growth, immigration and emigration, and finally, the Malthusian population doctrine, Wicksell came to what he called the two population questions.

The first one was formulated as follows (Wicksell, 1979: 146): '. . . which is, under given conditions, the optimal density of population in a country? Is the actual population under these conditions too large, about right, or too small, and which criteria could be used?' The optimum is 'the point where an increase of population would no longer in itself lead to any average increase in welfare but to the opposite' (Wicksell 1979: 146).[1] Wicksell pointed out that the optimum question is a purely economic question of great theoretical and practical importance. When the population grows, two opposing forces are at work. The first one is diminishing returns, which tend to lower per capita income, and the second is 'the united human efforts, the division of labor, the cooperation, the organization of industry, etc. . . . At the point where these tendencies cancel each other out is indeed the true optimum population' (Overbeek, 1973: 510).

Wicksell was completely convinced that the optimum had been exceeded everywhere in Europe (Wicksell, 1979: 146):

> For my own part, I have gradually reached the conviction that this optimum has already been considerably exceeded in our own country as in all countries of Europe, so that the road to increased prosperity does not lie in any further increase of population but rather in an energetic reduction of the population, continued through decades. . . . However strange such a thought may at first seem, it is nevertheless an almost self-evident conclusion as soon as one consistently embraces the general point of view of the Malthusian doctrine.

The second population question was: '. . . in what way should the equilibrium between births and deaths, if it is necessary or desirable, be achieved and maintained?' (Wicksell, 1979: 147). This, Wicksell argued (1979: 147), is not just an economic question but 'it touches on a great number of other social concerns' as well. 'Whether a population is dense or sparse, numerous or scanty, it must in the fullness of time become stationary, and even when growth is possible or desirable it will, at least in countries of old culture, necessarily fall short of the physiologically possible rate of growth' (Wicksell, 1979: 147–8).

Underpopulation?

The desirability of a reduction of the population came back in an article from 1914 (Wicksell, 1999b) where Wicksell discussed whether it is possible for a country to have too few inhabitants. His point of departure was the negative connotations for most of his contemporaries of the word depopulation (Wicksell, 1999b: 125):

> ... considered to stand self-condemned as being exceedingly injurious to the country, and pernicious.
>
> And yet of course a moment's reflection is enough to tell us that depopulation can often be a highly beneficial and even necessary thing – whenever, that is, a country's population, by the force of circumstances, has become excessively large. And that it *can* become too large surely no one can deny without being prepared to reject the evidence of all history.

Wicksell pointed out that there was only one example of modern depopulation of a country, that of Ireland, after the famine of the 1840s. By 1914, Ireland's population had been cut in half. 'But surely no reasonable person can blame or even pity the people of Ireland for this fact' (Wicksell, 1999b: 125). On the contrary, Wicksell (1999b: 125–6) painted a vivid and terrifying picture of what the population reduction allowed Ireland to avoid:[2]

> I believe it is Cliffe Leslie, the well-known economist, who tells stories from his youth about the horrific scenes in Ireland at that time, of which he was an eye-witness. Whole families lay dead of starvation or famine-fever in their miserable mud-hovels, and either because there was no time for burial in the usual sense of the word, or else people were afraid of infection, compassionate neighbours would climb up on the roof of the hovel and trample the whole thing down, turning it into both a grave and a monument to its unfortunate inhabitants. Compared with such scenes, Ireland's present condition can be seen as a golden age.

According to Wicksell, there are two main reasons why parents limit their offspring: the desire to provide an education and the desire not to divide the inheritance too many ways. The former simply indicates an imperfection in the way society handles education. The second reason, in turn, builds on the assumption that it is ownership of land and capital that constitutes the main difference between opulent and poor. The situation, however, Wicksell argued, would be completely different in a society with a stationary population, for there land rents and the return on capital would be drastically reduced, whereas wages would be much higher (Wicksell, 1999b: 128–9):

In a word: the national product per capita would be greatly increased by all these factors working in combination, but at the same time, *labour* would now become the main factor in the creation of value, and the 'product of labour' would accrue to those who worked. On this assumption, parents' worries about their children's future would naturally be greatly alleviated, particularly if the public authorities . . . were to assume greater responsibility than at present for the instruction and training of the young for their future vocations: no one who was in a position to provide society with bright, healthy children would be deterred from doing so by private economic motives. In a word, we would acquire a new condition of social equality at a far higher level of prosperity than at present, but without any tendency to put that prosperity at risk again by either too high or too low a birth rate.

Wicksell finished the article by examining some comparative statistics with respect to the relation between the population and the means of production in a number of countries – France, Italy, Germany, Austria– Hungary, Switzerland, Belgium, Germany, Britain, Russia, Japan, and Sweden – and concludes that in all these cases a reduction of the population would be called for.

The optimum population was a static concept. As time went by, Wicksell who at the beginning of the 1880s had recommended a slow increase of the Swedish population, became more and more convinced that the population had to be stationary instead. (Presumably this was what led him to the optimum population concept.) In an unfinished manuscript from 1924 or 1925 he took issue with the use of the concept 'normal population growth,' advocating instead his old idea from the French prize essay (Wicksell, 1924/25: 260):

Who has not heard about 'the normal growth of populations' and the necessity to maintain this, and yet this expression is an obvious self-contradiction, since *every* population growth percentage that does not practically coincide with standstill is an unconditionally *abnormal* phenomenon in the sense that it can only take place during shorter time periods, whereas the *normal* [situation] must be either a stationary population or else – as was mainly the case in olden days – a fluctuation between growth and decrease around an approximately unchanged equilibrium.

The light at the end of the tunnel

Toward the end of his life, Wicksell thought that he could see some progress in the struggle for a smaller population. One of his last pamphlets, and one of his last publications altogether, on the procreation issue (Wicksell, 1925), dealt with the purpose of Malthusianism: 'the system of regulated fertility' (Wicksell, 1925: 3). Wicksell listed three different purposes. The first is to make each individual couple of parents able to further their well-being and that of their children better. The second is to put the size of the population into a better relation with the economic resources of the country than when procreation is unhampered, as this would both increase per capita income and reduce the income gap between rich and poor. Finally, adhering to the neo-Malthusian canon would increase the moral standard of the entire population (Wicksell, 1925: 4):

> It seeks – for the first time in world history with a possibility of success – to fight prostitution and all other sexual perversions and calamities by providing an opportunity for a sound, natural, and hence happy and virtuous, life, also sexually, for each sexually mature individual.

Wicksell noted with satisfaction that considerable progress had been made with respect to the limitation of the size of the individual family: 'The unnaturally large number of children and the even larger number of births that were formerly very common also among the educated and better-off classes, in our time remain a rare thing also among the working class' (Wicksell, 1925: 4). He was happy to see that it was seldom that more than two or three children were found, however, mainly in the capital, whereas 'in the rest of the country it may not be so well, above all not in upper Norrland, where the population still seems to be living the very primitive life of nature' (Wicksell, 1925: 5). Still, he was able to conclude that considerable progress had been made.

The size of the overall population, on the other hand, still left a lot to be desired. It was not enough that each individual family managed to bring the number of births down, because *pari passu* with the declining birth rate there had been a reduction in the death rate, and Sweden may very well have had a tremendous overpopulation were it not for emigration above all to the United States. That safety valve was virtually closed in 1925. Still, Wicksell was optimistic, as the reduction in the birth rate had been so substantial during the preceding decades 'that a real regulation of the population appears to be in sight, even independently of the possibility of continued emigration' (Wicksell, 1925: 6). Three years earlier, he had reported to the Fifth International Neo-Malthusian and Birth Control Conference, held in London, on the progress made in Sweden (Hashimoto, forthcoming, Letter 176):

... the present number of children born in Sweden is so small that when they come to the age of twenty they will not be able even to supplant the present number of men and women in the twenties, so that our population in that respect may already be regarded as *virtually* stationary.

Wicksell pointed to Germany as an example for Sweden. In Germany, the birth rate, which had been 'even phenomenally high' (Wicksell, 1925: 6) after the Franco-Prussian War, had dropped rapidly. Wicksell predicted that this would continue until Germany would reach a new and better economic equilibrium at a lower population size, and he went on to project the same development in the rest of Western Europe. One of the most important consequences would be that the probability of war in Europe would be drastically reduced. 'On my part, I view such a possibility with unmixed joy, already as a guarantee for the maintenance of peace in our continent' (Wicksell, 1925: 9). How wrong he would be.

The one and only remedy

When it came to the methods for reducing the size of the population, Wicksell was opposed to postponing the age at which marriage was contracted. This age was already too high in Sweden, he argued, and the Swedes entered fewer marital unions than other Europeans. Postponing them further yet would simply breed drunkenness and prostitution. The alternative was celibacy, but in the struggle between celibacy and prostitution the former in general pulled the short straw. From Drysdale, Wicksell had accepted 'the ... reasonable idea that abstinence generally produces nervous disturbances,' as Gårdlund (1996: 57) puts it. In a pamphlet on prostitution from 1887 (Wicksell, 1887b: 48–9), he wrote:

> But a non-prejudiced look at reality must lead everyone to the view [. . .] that a regular satisfaction of the sexual instinct, as offered by marriage, and beginning at the time of reaching sexual maturity for most males constitutes an essential, for many even an indispensable, condition for the preservation of the health of mind and body, and the only completely reliable defense against aberrations of a more or less sad, more or less destructive kind.

Wicksell refuted the idea that the sexual instinct was mainly dysfunctional in contemporary society with its prevailing values. It could not be argued that although it may have served primitive man in his perennial fights against enemies by ensuring the survival of mankind, in Wicksell's own time it was simply one of the worst scourges that it was impossible to get rid of, despite all prayers and efforts expended. Instead, it was one of 'the richest sources of a harmonious and happy existence. All that we can do is to regulate this instinct so that it does not become an obstacle to the welfare of mankind; this then becomes the aim of rational morality' (Wicksell, 1882: 73). The only remedy was the neo-Malthusian one. In this, Wicksell claimed, he had Jesus and Paul on his side.

The same view came back in the booklet on population. Wicksell (1979: 149–50) refuted the view held by Charles Darwin that 'positive' Malthusian checks on the population may not be altogether negative, as without them mankind might possibly degenerate and decline. He also refuted Malthus' recommendation that marriages ought to be postponed for a couple of years on average. Following this advice would simply make life unbearable. In the prostitution pamphlet, Wicksell (1887b: 44) had made completely clear what he thought about it:

> ... the demands made on the contemporary youth when it comes to morality certainly do not have any parallel in any previous age. At the present low frequency of marriage, lower in our own country than in any other country in Europe, what is actually demanded (and this is the case especially for the educated classes in society) not only from a young man or two, but from virtually all, that all the way up to their thirtieth year and beyond that they shall live in strict celibacy. It is demanded of them that during the most beautiful and powerful years of their youth, when the drives and urges are most potent, they should as *one* man subject themselves to the strongest asceticism of monastic life, and this even though it will be difficult to find any great number among them with the religious enthusiasm which once must have supported life within the monasteries.

Thus there was little choice 'besides the neomalthusian programme: early marriage but few children – on average 2–3 to a family – and, for the rest, voluntary sterility' (Wicksell, 1979: 150). Early marriages were not feasible when they, 'as is too often the case' were 'synonymous with the procreation of an unlimited, uncontrolled number of new individuals' (Wicksell, 1887b: 49).

Wicksell was deeply concerned with the effects of too rapid population growth on the morality of the nation. He was worried about the decreasing frequency of marriages, especially among young people. The absence of an orderly family life would simply lead to an increase in the incidence of prostitution and in the number of children born out of wedlock. In a way, prostitution contributed to a reduction of the population growth.

'*Prostitution is sterile*' wrote Wicksell (1887a: 32) in 1887, both because the women practicing it in the end become less prone to bear children but also because their male customers will not produce as numerous an offspring as they would have if they had married instead. Again he directed a plea to the medical profession to help their patients in matters related to conception, and recommend the study of an anonymous pamphlet, written by his friend Hjalmar Öhrvall: *Försigtighetsmått i ägtenskapet* (*Precautionary Measures in Married Life*), prefaced by himself (Öhrvall, 1886).

He reiterated his views in an unpublished article from 1921. The only way of getting rid of prostitution was by allowing contraceptive devices to be used within the family. 'Prostitution is *sterile*. This is its only but terribly strong *raison d'être*. If you do not dare to fight it with its own weapons, i.e. facultative sterility within the matrimony, it is invincible' (Wicksell, 1921c: 248). The best way to combat prostitution was by making sexual relations within the marriage possible without risk for unwanted pregnancies. 'Our ideal should ... be: wife, mother and lover in the person of the same woman, and this can be realized, but only through voluntary sterility to the full extent required' (Wicksell, 1925: 17).

Later in his life, Wicksell would go one step further in his view of how to limit population growth and argue that women should have the right to abortion under reasonable circumstances. A court case of abortion in 1916, which led to conviction, prompted him to draft an article (never published during his lifetime), in which he put the abortion issue into a historical perspective and pointed out that during ancient times no prohibition existed. It was not mentioned in the Bible, and Plato and Aristotle recommended both abortion and infanticide as suitable means for keeping the size of the population within tolerable limits. Wicksell discussed how these views changed and the role of the Christian church in this, and argued that the legal punishments meted out for illegal abortion were far too hard, bearing little relation to the severity of the crime. Society either had to support the mothers economically to make it possible for them to bring up their children, or put the necessary means for avoiding unwanted pregnancies at their disposal (Wicksell, 1916a). Four years later, Wicksell argued that until means had been developed that were completely effective when it came to prevent conception, *all* punishments for both the physician and the woman in case of abortion had better be abolished (Wicksell, 1921c: 248).

That, Wicksell suggested, also raised the question of whether abortion should be *permitted*. 'This is certainly a most delicate question, and personally it is only at an advanced age that I have been able to overcome the apprehension that already the nature of the issue and even more an inherited tradition raise against it' (Wicksell, 1925: 17). He recommended the formulation of an explicit set of criteria that could be used to determine when abortion should be allowed and not. The simplest rule would be to allow it to take place freely, e.g. before the third month of pregnancy when the movement of the fetus begins. The main route to a regulation of fertility, he concluded, should be through the use of contraceptives and the role of abortion should be that of 'an available *last resort*, a safe *guarantee* for the many that absolutely need [it]' (Wicksell, 1925: 24).

8 Wicksell's views

A summary interpretation

If we caricature a little, the way in which Wicksell's views on population and poverty are usually conceived is the following. The sex drive of mankind leads it to reproduce in geometric progression, as hypothesized by Malthus. Food production, on the other hand, only increases in arithmetic progression, also à la Malthus. This is an unsustainable situation, which can last for a limited time only. People get poorer and then attempt to emigrate if they can. For those who fail, the vices of drunkenness and prostitution lurk around the corner. The only escape goes through the systematic use of contraceptives within the marriage. The optimum population is the one that maximizes the economic well-being of the population. 'The optimum population theory is the core of Wicksell's population theory,' summarizes Monica Fong (1976: 315). This is usually the only credit he receives when his writings on population are mentioned.

This treatment is not fair to Wicksell, for his ideas link up nicely in a general equilibrium framework of international trade and factor movements. In his foreword to *Value, Capital and Rent*, G. L. S. Shackle (1954: 7) makes the following characteristic of Wicksell's scientific contribution: 'Wicksell's work was like a mountain from whose flanks divergent streams run down and bring fertility to widely separate fields, only to merge again later into a single broad river.' This statement describes his views on poverty and population very well. In order to get a complete picture of them we must pull a number of threads together. The present chapter is devoted to a demonstration of how this can be done.

A formalization of the Wicksellian system

Wicksell's discussion of the effects of population growth is carried out within an implicit framework that closely resembles the modern general equilibrium approach to international trade and factor movements, as this had been developed in the 1970s. Time after time he comes back to the interplay between events in Europe and overseas. In the present context we will label these two regions 'The Old World' and 'The New World' respectively. The production structure that Wicksell worked with is almost completely symmetric. Both regions produce agricultural goods on the one hand and manufactures on the other. (Below we will come back to the main difference: the temporary existence of an agricultural frontier in the New World.) Let us begin by portraying the Old World.

The production functions of the Old World are:

$$A_O = A_O (L_{OA}, \bar{T}_O, \bar{K}_{OA}) \tag{8.1}$$

$$M_O = M_O (L_{OM}, \bar{R}_O, \bar{K}_{OM}) \tag{8.2}$$

which are both assumed to linearly homogeneous, with diminishing returns to all production factors, but with positive cross-derivatives. Production of agricultural goods (A_O) takes place with the aid of labor (L_{OA}), land (T_O) and capital (K_{OA}), whereas manufacturing (M_O) uses labor (L_{OM}), a natural resource (R_O), e.g. the Swedish forests or mineral ores, and capital (K_{OM}). Labor is mobile between the two sectors, and there is full employment of the labor force (L_O):

$$L_{OA} + L_{OM} = L_O \tag{8.3}$$

The extension of the land area is given and all land suitable for agricultural production is under the plow. Land is thus a fixed production factor. So is the natural resource. As we found in the chapter on diminishing returns, Wicksell kept insisting on the exhaustibility of natural resources everywhere. He did not deal with mobility of capital anywhere in his writings on population and poverty. In fact, the importance of capital in agriculture is played down almost everywhere, except in his discussion of technological progress. This makes it reasonable to treat the two capital stocks as sector specific. It is thus obvious that Wicksell's production framework essentially corresponds to the specific factors model of Ronald Jones (1971), with a single mobile factor: labor (see also Samuelson, 1971a,b).

With profit-maximizing producers in both sectors, the production factors are rewarded with the value of their respective marginal products. If we choose to use manufactures as our *numéraire*, i.e. set $P_M = 1$ and $P = P_A/P_M$, we must have that:

$$w_O = PA_O{}^L \tag{8.4}$$

$$w_0 = M_0{}^L \tag{8.5}$$

for the wage rate. With sector-specific factors, there will be no factor price equalization between countries. The easiest way to see this is by borrowing a diagram from the original Jones (1971) article.

In Figure 8.1 we have put the two Old World curves for the value of the marginal productivity (VMPL) in agriculture and manufacturing back to back. Labor use in agriculture is measured leftward from O and labor use in manufacturing rightward from the same point. Assume that the total labor force available is AB. Dividing this between the two sectors so as to equalize the VMPL, yields an Old World wage rate equal to OE. The figure has been drawn on the assumption of given capital stocks, land, and natural resources. Assume next that the New World has exactly the same the same technology and endowments of the fixed factors as the Old World, so that the same VMPL curves apply, but a labor force which is only equal to $A'B'$. This will then give rise to a higher wage rate in the New World: OF. Thus, as long as migration is not free, neither the wages nor the returns to the specific factors will be equalized. Hence we need to operate with one wage rate (w_O) for the Old World and one (w_N) for the New World.

Turning to the returns to the specific factors we have:

$$r_{OA} = PA_0{}^T \tag{8.6}$$

for the land rent,

$$r_{OM} = M_0{}^R \tag{8.7}$$

for the natural resource rent, and

$$i_{OA} = PA_0{}^K \tag{8.8}$$

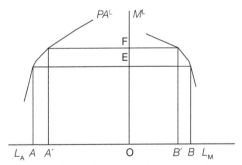

Figure 8.1 Wage determination in the specific factors model.

$$i_{OM} = M_O^K \tag{8.9}$$

for the returns to the two capital stocks.

The outputs of the two commodities can also be expressed as functions of their relative price (P) and a shift parameter (α), to symbolize exogenous influences on production, such as changes in factor endowments and technology:

$$A_O = A_O(P, \alpha) \tag{8.10}$$

$$M_O = M_O(P, \alpha) \tag{8.11}$$

Wicksell discusses changes in demand and relative commodity prices, i.e. he works with the assumption of two 'large' economic regions whose actions together determine international prices. This means that we have to specify the demand side as well. The total income of the Old World (Y_O) is given by:

$$Y_O = PA_O + M_O \tag{8.12}$$

This entire income is spent on consumption of the two goods (D_{OA} and D_{OM}):

$$Y_O = PD_{OA} + D_{OM} \tag{8.13}$$

The demand for agricultural goods in the Old World is a function of relative commodity prices, income and preferences (symbolized by the shift parameter β):

$$D_{OA} = D_{OA}(P, Y_O, \beta) \tag{8.14}$$

This finishes our description of the Old World. The economic structure of the New World is completely analogous (however, see below for the case of the agrarian frontier) but for the separate shift parameters, γ and δ (and hence the equations are numbered analogously):

$$A_N = A_N(L_{NA}, \bar{T}_N, \bar{K}_{NA}) \tag{8.1'}$$

$$M_N = M_N(L_{NM}, \bar{R}_N, \bar{K}_{NM}) \tag{8.2'}$$

$$L_{NA} + L_{NM} = L_N \tag{8.3'}$$

$$w_N = PA_N^L \tag{8.4'}$$

$$w_N = M_N^L \tag{8.5'}$$

$$r_{NA} = PA_N^T \tag{8.6'}$$

$$r_{NM} = M_N^R \tag{8.7'}$$

$$i_{NA} = PA_N^K \tag{8.8'}$$

$$i_{NM} = M_N^K \tag{8.9'}$$

$$A_N = A_N(P, \gamma) \tag{8.10'}$$

$$M_N = M_N(P, \gamma) \tag{8.11'}$$

$$Y_N = PA_N + M_N \tag{8.12'}$$

$$Y_N = PD_{NA} + D_{NM} \tag{8.13'}$$

$$D_{NA} = D_{NA}(P, Y_N, \delta) \tag{8.14'}$$

What remains to be done is to close the system: Wicksell assumes that the Old World trades freely with the New World (while factor movements are regulated). Thus we may use the equilibrium condition for the market for agricultural goods:

$$D_{OA} - A_O = A_N - D_{NA} \tag{8.15}$$

where the Old World is a net importer and the New World a net exporter, as is clear from the chapter on trade. No corresponding equation is needed for the market for manufactures, as according to Walras' law, if all markets except one are in equilibrium then the last one must be so too.

The system (8.3)–(8.14), (8.3')–(8.14') and (8.15) has twenty-five equations and twenty-five unknowns (A_O, M_O, L_{OA}, L_{OM}, w_O, r_{OA}, r_{OM}, i_{OA}, i_{OM}, Y_O, D_{OA}, D_{OM}, the corresponding New World variables and P). This system can be used for studying the parameter changes in Wicksell's system, and the production functions (8.1)–(8.2) and (8.1')–(8.2') can be used for solving for output changes at given commodity prices.

The effects of population growth in the Old World

The trigger that puts the Wicksellian system in motion is the human sex drive, which results in the growth of the population and the labor force in the Old World. With given relative commodity prices, this will serve to increase employment and production in both sectors, lower the wage rate and increase the returns to all the fixed factors. To see this, we employ equations (8.3)–(8.5) to solve for changes in employment and wages, (8.1)–(8.2) to solve for output changes, and finally (8.6)–(8.9) to find the changes in the rewards of the specific factors.

Differentiating (8.3)–(8.5) yields:

$$dL_{OA} + dL_{OM} = dL_O \qquad (8.16)$$

$$dw_O = PA_O^{LL} dL_{OA} \qquad (8.17)$$

$$dw_O = M_O^{LL} dL_{OM} \qquad (8.18)$$

and

$$dL_{OA} = -(1/\Delta) M_O^{LL} dL_O > 0 \qquad (8.19)$$

$$dL_{OM} = -(1/\Delta) PA_O^{LL} dL_O > 0 \qquad (8.20)$$

where

$$\Delta = -(M_O^{LL} + PA_O^{LL}) > 0 \qquad (8.21)$$

and $dw_O < 0$, from (8.4) or (8.5).

Differentiating (8.1) and (8.2) gives:

$$dA_O = A_O^L dL_{OA} > 0 \qquad (8.22)$$

$$dM_O = M_O^L dL_{OM} > 0 \qquad (8.23)$$

These changes portray the basic Malthusian mechanism. When the population and the labor force grow, at constant commodity prices, both agriculture and manufacturing increase their employment of labor, but only at a falling wage rate in terms of manufactures, and hence increase their output as well. It is easily demonstrated that this simultaneously increases the returns to the fixed factors, e.g. the land rent. Differentiating (8.6) gives:

$$dr_{OA} = PA_0^{TL}dL_{OA} > 0 \qquad (8.24)$$

This is what Wicksell meant when he stated that the rich in society – the owners of fixed assets – had an interest in maintaining a high rate of population growth, whereas at the same time this served to depress the living standard of the workers, i.e. to increase their poverty. That, in turn, was what led to drunkenness and other social evils.

Technological progress

As we found in Chapter 4, Wicksell did not believe that technological progress could serve to overcome the effects of diminishing returns. Let us examine what the effects of technological progress may be with given commodity prices. This makes it possible to compare directly with the effects of population growth. Differentiating equations (8.3)–(8.5) with a constant population and labor force gives:

$$dL_{OA} + dL_{OM} = 0 \qquad (8.25)$$

$$dw_0 = P(A_0^{LL}dL_{OA} + A_0^{L\alpha}d\alpha) \qquad (8.26)$$

$$dw_0 = M_0^{LL}dL_{OM} + M_0^{L\alpha}d\alpha \qquad (8.27)$$

where $d\alpha$ symbolizes technological progress, $A_0^{L\alpha}$ and $M_0^{L\alpha}$ measure the impact of technological progress on the marginal productivity of labor in agriculture and manufacturing, respectively. This gives the following solutions for labor use and wages:

$$dL_{OA} = (1/\Delta)(PA_0^{L\alpha} - M_0^{L\alpha})d\alpha \qquad (8.28)$$

$$dL_{OM} = (1/\Delta)(M_0^{L\alpha} - PA_0^{L\alpha})d\alpha = -dL_{OA} \qquad (8.29)$$

$$dw_0 = -(1/\Delta)P(A_0^{LL}M_0^{L\alpha} + M_0^{LL}A_0^{L\alpha})d\alpha > 0 \qquad (8.30)$$

where Δ is our (8.21).

We find that provided that both marginal productivities are increased by technological progress then the wage rate must rise. As we know, however,

Wicksell also discusses the case where technological progress may *decrease* the marginal productivity of labor. If this happens in both sectors, the wage rate must fall, and should it be the case in one of the two sectors, the outcome for the wage rate will depend on the relative magnitudes of the changes. Whether labor moves in or out of agriculture (manufacturing) in the 'normal' case where both marginal products are increased by technological progress depends on which of the two productivity-increasing effects is the stronger one.

We can now compare the effects of diminishing returns on the wage rate with those of technological progress. This is done in (8.31) where both the growth of the labor force and technological progress have been incorporated:

$$dw_O = -(1/\Delta)P[A_O^{LL}M_O^{LL}dL_O + (A_O^{LL}M_O^{L\alpha} + M_O^{LL}A_O^{L\alpha})d\alpha] \qquad (8.31)$$

What Wicksell argues is that the first term within the square brackets is larger than the last. The sizes of the labor force growth, dL_O, and the strength of the diminishing returns, A_O^{LL} and M_O^{LL}, are strong enough to outweigh the productivity-raising influences of technological progress, $M_O^{L\alpha}$ and $A_O^{L\alpha}$.

Assuming that the above sequence is generalized to the entire Old World, it is bound to have an impact on relative commodity prices as well. In order to find the direction of the price change, however, we must make use of the larger general equilibrium system above. We then need the supply functions for the two goods in the Old and the New Worlds, (8.10)–(8.11) and (8.10')–(8.11'), the two regional income expressions (8.12) and (8.12'), the two demand functions for agricultural goods, (8.14 and 8.14'), and, finally, the equilibrium condition for the market for agricultural goods: (8.15). This system of nine equations can be solved for changes in the nine unknowns A_O, M_O, A_N, M_N, Y_O, Y_N, D_{OA}, D_{NA}, and P. Differentiating the system, assuming that no technological change takes place and that there is no exogenous change in the New World, and solving for dP yields:

$$dP = -(1/\Delta^*)[D_{OA}^{\beta}d\beta - D_{OA}^{Y}P(A_O^{\alpha}-M_O^{LL} + M_O^{\alpha}-A_O^{LL})(1/\Delta)dL_O$$
$$+ PA_O^{\alpha}-M_O^{LL}(1/\Delta)dL_O] \qquad (8.32)$$

where

$$\Delta^* = D_{OA}^{P} + D_{OA}^{Y}A_O + D_{OA}^{Y}(PA_O^{P} + M_O^{P}) + D_{NA}^{P}$$
$$+ D_{NA}^{Y}A_N + D_{NA}^{Y}(PA_N^{P} + M_N^{P}) - A_O^{P} - A_N^{P} < 0 \qquad (8.33)$$

where we have used (8.19) and (8.20) and $\Delta > 0$ is our (8.21).

The denominator (8.33) must be negative. This is nothing but the partial derivative of the excess demand for agricultural goods with respect to their price, and if our model is to be stable in the sense of Walras, this must be negative. The numerator in turn contains three terms. The first is the change in the demand for agricultural goods in the Old World that results from a change in preferences at given incomes and commodity prices when the population grows. Wicksell envisaged an increased demand for food (agricultural goods) when the population grew. This he made explicit in the case of the New World, where it 'also' took place, and it is clear that he had the same mechanism in mind for the Old World. Hence, this term is positive.

The second term is the increased demand for agricultural goods that emanates from the increase of the total income of the Old World when the labor force grows and more of both commodities is produced at given prices. Assuming that agricultural goods are not inferior then this term should be positive as well. The third term is the increase in the production of agricultural goods that takes place when the labor force grows as a result of population growth, and this term pulls in the opposite direction. Whether the relative price of agricultural goods rises or falls then depends exclusively on whether the demand for agricultural goods increases faster than the supply of it when the population grows in the Old World. Wicksell assumed that the demand effect was the strongest one. Thus, population growth at home tends to turn the terms of trade against the Old World.

Problems of foreign trade

Wicksell did not believe that a specialization according to comparative advantage would contribute to solving the population problem in the Old World. On the contrary, he argued, there were least three problems connected with international trade that would preclude it from working as an engine (Robertson, 1938), or even as a 'handmaiden' (Kravis, 1970) of growth, to use two latter-day terms. The first was the tendency for manufacturing output to stagnate in the Old World when natural resources were depleted. The second was the tariff policy of the New World (read: the United States). The third was population growth and demand changes in the New World. Let us see how this works in terms of our model.

The depletion of natural resources can be expressed as a reduction of R_O, i.e. $dR_O < 0$. Differentiating (8.3)–(8.5) once more, but this time with a given labor force, yields:

$$dL_{OA} + dL_{OM} = 0 \tag{8.34}$$

$$dw_O = PA_O{}^{LL}dL_{OA} \tag{8.35}$$

$$dw_O = M_O{}^{LR}dR_O + M_O{}^{LL}dL_{OM} \tag{8.36}$$

and

$$dL_{OA} = -dL_{OM} = -(1/\Delta)M_O{}^{LR}dR_O > 0 \tag{8.37}$$

$$dw_O = -(1/\Delta)PA_O{}^{LL}M_O{}^{LR}dR_O < 0 \tag{8.38}$$

where $dR_O < 0$ and Δ is still (8.21).

When the natural resource shrinks, the marginal productivity of labor is reduced in manufacturing, and this sector hence starts to shed workers, who can only be reabsorbed in the economy – some of them in agriculture – at a lower wage rate. This also means that manufacturing output must contract while agricultural output expands:

$$dM_O = M_O{}^{R}dR_O + M_O{}^{L}dL_{OM} < 0 \tag{8.39}$$

$$dA_O = A_O{}^{L}dL_{OA} = -A_O{}^{L}dL_{OM} > 0 \tag{8.40}$$

At the same time, with given commodity prices, Y_O must fall, as the total factor endowment of the Old World has shrunk:

$$dY_O = -PA_O{}^{L}dL_{OM} + M_O{}^{R}dR_O + M_O{}^{L}dL_{OM} \tag{8.41}$$

but as

$$PA_O{}^{L} = M_O{}^{L} = w_O \tag{8.42}$$

(8.41) reduces to

$$dY_O = M_O{}^{R}dR_O < 0 \tag{8.43}$$

Provided that neither of the two goods is inferior, the demand for both manufactures and agricultural goods must shrink as income shrinks, i.e. the relative price of agricultural goods, whose production has increased, must fall in relation to that of manufactures. As Wicksell predicted, the depletion of natural resources tends to reduce the demand for imports in the Old

World, as this region can now afford to buy less. This in turn interacts with the changes on the supply side to reduce the relative price of agricultural goods in the world market.

The second problem for the Old World when it comes to using international trade to mitigate the consequences of population growth, according to Wicksell, was the tendency for the New World countries (notably the United States) to use tariffs to protect their manufacturing sectors. Tariffs drive a wedge between relative commodity prices in the domestic market in the New World and world market prices (still adhered to in the Old World). We may denote the former by P_N, while retaining P for the relative world market price of agricultural goods. This means that we have to add an equation to our general equilibrium system:

$$P_N = P_A/P_M(1 + t) = P/(1 + t) \tag{8.44}$$

or

$$P = P_N(1 + t) \tag{8.45}$$

where t is the tariff on manufactures in the New World. Let us next find out what the introduction of the tariff will do to P_N and P.

Let us begin with the former. We then need equations (8.10)–(8.12), (8.14), (8.10′)–(8.12′), (8.14′) – the last modified so as to incorporate P_N instead of P – plus (8.15) and (8.45). Differentiating this system, assuming that initially $P_N = P$, and $t = 0$, and solving for dP_N yields:

$$dP_N = (1/\Delta^*)P[A_O^P - D_{OA}^P - D_{OA}^Y A_O - D_{OA}^Y(PA_O^P + M_O^P)]dt < 0 \tag{8.46}$$

where $\Delta^* < 0$, is (8.33) above. The introduction of the tariff on manufactured goods raises the relative price of these goods in the New World, i.e. it lowers the price of agricultural goods in terms of manufactures. Expression (8.46) shows that when the tariff on manufactures is introduced in the New World, if we keep P_N constant, the relative price of agricultural goods must increase in the world market (cf. 8.45). Old World producers then react by increasing their production and Old World consumers reduce their demand (whereas New World consumers and producers, who are facing P_N, not P, do not react at all). An excess supply is created, which serves to lower the price of agricultural goods in the New World.

To find out what happens to the world market price, P, we use (8.44) instead of (8.45), together with the other equations employed in the derivation of (8.46). This yields:

$$dP = (1/\Delta^*)P[D_{NA}{}^P + D_{NA}{}^Y A_N + D_{NA}{}^Y (PA_N{}^P + M_N{}^P) - A_N{}^P]dt > 0 \quad (8.47)$$

by analogy with (8.46). This expression must be positive, as the denominator is negative and the numerator is the partial derivative of the excess *demand* for agricultural goods with respect to its price, which, for stability reasons, must be negative. Thus, a tariff on manufactured goods in the New World will lower its relative price in the world market, i.e. increase the relative price of agricultural goods.

When the tariff is introduced, if we keep P constant, the relative domestic price of agricultural goods in the New World falls (cf. 8.44). New World consumers increase their demand and producers reduce their supply. An excess demand is created in the world market and the international price of agricultural good rises.

Together, (8.46) and (8.47) express a standard result: when a tariff is introduced in a large open economy, this serves to increase the domestic price of the good subject to the tariff, whereas it will lower its price in the world market. The tariff pulls resources out of agriculture into manufacturing in the New World, and hence reduces the worldwide supply of agricultural goods.

The third of Wicksell's obstacles to international trade is the rising demand for agricultural goods that accompanies the growth of the population in the New World. This is obtained by differentiating (8.14′) with commodity prices and incomes held constant:

$$dD_{NA} = D_{NA}{}^\delta d\delta \quad (8.48)$$

This works exactly as $D_{OA}{}^\beta d\beta$ in (8.32). It serves to increase the relative price of agricultural goods in the world market, i.e. it tends to turn the terms of trade against the Old World. It should, however, be noted that it does not work in isolation but is a result of the growth of the population in the New World, which means that its effects, and the effects of rising New World income, must be weighed against the effects of increased New World production of agricultural goods when the labor force of the New World grows. Let us next turn to the investigation of these effects, but then we must also introduce emigration from the Old to the New World.

Migration from the Old to the New World

The fall in the wage rate in the Old World when the population there grows is what triggers emigration for Wicksell. The effect of this is to increase the population in the New World instead of in the Old. Hence, it is part of the sequence we have just discussed. In the New World it increases the demand for agricultural goods at given commodity prices and incomes, it increases the production of agricultural goods, and it increases income and hence the demand for agricultural goods at constant commodity prices.

In his discussion of agricultural production in the New World, Wicksell kept coming back to the issue of the land frontier. This frontier, he argued, was rapidly being closed, at least in the United States, while it might still be in existence elsewhere in the New World. Our general equilibrium model can be used to examine both situations. Let us begin with the case where emigrants who arrive in the New World can put virgin land under the plow.

For the sake of simplicity, let us assume that the entire addition to the Old World population can emigrate to the New World. (This allows us to disregard production effects in the Old World.) When they arrive at their new destination they can either work in the manufacturing sector or in agriculture, on the existing agricultural land. They may also, however, extend the land frontier. The concept of an endogenous land frontier has been explored in different settings by Ronald Findlay (1993; 1995, chapter 5) and by Findlay and myself (Findlay and Lundahl, 1994). These formulations, however, all rest upon the use of capital for extending the frontier. In the present context we will instead draw on another Findlay (1996) model, of the territorial expansion of empires, in which it is the use of labor (an army) that extends the territory. Here we may think of a land-clearing 'brigade' (L_{NT}) instead, as this is clearly how Wicksell conceived of the situation.

The introduction of an endogenous land frontier changes the production function for agricultural goods in the New World to:

$$A_N = A_N[L_{NA}, T_N(L_{NT}), \bar{K}_{NA}] \tag{8.1''}$$

Labor now has to be divided between three different uses:

$$L_{NA} + L_{NM} + L_{NT} = L_N \tag{8.3''}$$

and to the two wage equations (8.4′) and (8.5′) we have to add a third one:

$$w_N = PA_N{}^T T^L \tag{8.49}$$

We will furthermore assume that on the frontier land can be obtained only at an increasing cost in terms of labor, i.e. that the clearing of land is subject to diminishing returns ($T^L > 0$, $T^{LL} < 0$).

Differentiating (8.3″), (8.4′), (8.5′), and (8.49) yields:

$$dL_{NA} + dL_{NM} + dL_{NT} = dL_N \tag{8.50}$$

$$dw_N = P(A_N^{LL}dL_{NA} + A_N^{LT}T^L dL_{NT}) \tag{8.51}$$

$$dw_N = M_N^{LL}dL_{NM} \tag{8.52}$$

$$dw_N = P[(T^L)^2 A_N^{TT} + A_N^{T}T^{LL}]dL_{NT} + PT^L A_N^{TL}dL_{NA} \tag{8.53}$$

This system of four equations can now be solved for the changes in labor use and the change in the wage rate in the New World as new emigrants arrive:

$$dL_{NA} = (1/\Delta^{**})PM_N^{LL}[A_N^{TT}(T^L)^2 + A_N^{T}T^{LL} - A_N^{TL}T^L]dL_N > 0 \tag{8.54}$$

$$dL_{NM} = (1/\Delta^{**})P^2\{(T^L)^2[A_N^{TT}A_N^{LL} - (A_N^{TL})^2] \\ + A_N^{T}T^{LL}A_N^{LL}\}dL_N > 0 \tag{8.55}$$

$$dL_{NT} = (1/\Delta^{**})PM_N^{LL}(A_N^{LL} - A_N^{TL}T^L)dL_N > 0 \tag{8.56}$$

$$dw_N = (1/\Delta^{**})P^2 M_N^{LL}\{(T^L)^2[A_N^{TT}A_N^{LL} - (A_N^{TL})^2] \\ + A_N^{LL}A_N^{T}T^{LL}\}dL_N < 0 \tag{8.57}$$

where

$$\Delta^{**} = PM_N^{LL}[A_N^{TT}(T^L)^2 + A_N^{T}T^{LL} + A_N^{LL} - 2A_N^{TL}T^L] \\ + P^2\{A_N^{LL}A_N^{T}T^{LL} + (T^L)^2[A_N^{TT}A_N^{LL} - (A_N^{TL})^2]\} \tag{8.58}$$

and where we have used the fact that when production functions are linearly homogeneous, $A_N^{TL} = A_N^{LT}$.

The denominator Δ^{**} is positive. The first term is positive, so is the first part of the second, and we can prove that so is the last part as well. For this we use Euler's theorem. With linearly homogeneous production functions we have that

$$A_N^{TT}T_N + A_N^{LT}L_{NA} + A_N^{KT}K_{NA} \equiv 0 \tag{8.59}$$

$$A_N^{TL}T_N + A_N^{LL}L_{NA} + A_N^{KL}K \equiv 0 \tag{8.60}$$

Equations (8.59) and (8.60) may be solved for A_N^{TT} and A_N^{LL} respectively:

$$A_N^{TT} = -A_N^{LT}(L_{NA}/T_N) - A_N^{KL}(K_{NA}/T_N) \tag{8.61}$$

$$A_N^{LL} = -A_N^{TL}(T_N/L_{NA}) - A_N^{KL}(K_{NA}/L_{NA}) \tag{8.62}$$

These expressions can now be substituted into the last term of (8.58) and the expression within the second squared brackets may be developed to yield

$$A_N^{TT}A_N^{LL} - (A_N^{TL})^2 = A_N^{TL}A_N^{KL}(K_{NA}/T_N) + A_N^{KT}A_N^{TL}(K_{NA}/L_{NA})$$
$$+ A_N^{KT}A_N^{KL}(K_{NA}/T_N)(K_{NA}/L_{NA}) > 0 \tag{8.63}$$

Thus, the entire expression (8.58) is positive.

What happens when the emigrants arrive in the New World is that they go into all three employments: directly into agriculture, into manufacturing, and indirectly into agriculture by developing the marginal land so that it may be put under the plow. They can be absorbed, however, only at the cost of a falling wage rate.

It is also interesting to investigate what will happen to the land rent on the frontier. The land rent is given by (8.6′). Differentiating this, and keeping in mind that

$$T_N = T_N(L_{NT}) \tag{8.64}$$

yields

$$dr_{NA} = P(A_N^{TL}dL_{NA} + A_N^{TT}T^l dL_{NT}) \tag{8.65}$$

Inserting the expressions for the change in labor use (8.54) and (8.56) gives us

$$dr_{NA} = (1/\Delta^{**})P^2 M_N^{LL}\{T^L[A_N^{TT}A_N^{LL} - (A^{TL})^2] + A_N^{TL}A_N^T T^{LL}\}dL_N \tag{8.66}$$

The land rent will fall in the New World when immigrants arrive and cultivation is extended, unless diminishing returns to extension are strong. According to Wicksell, the frontier is virtually closed, so the latter is precisely what we should expect, and once the frontier is closed we are back in our original general equilibrium system. The analogy with (8.28)–(8.30) is perfect, with the one difference that the New World has a higher endowment of land, which should mean that the existing wage rate is higher there than in the Old World, as pointed out by Wicksell and illustrated in Figure 8.1. Emigration should thus be beneficial for those who undertake it. Also, as far as the development of relative commodity prices is concerned, (8.32) may be used, substituting N (the New World) for O (the Old World).

Presumably, however, the tendency for population growth to increase the relative price of agricultural goods is weaker when the population grows in the New World instead of in the Old, as the additional agricultural output generated should be higher and the shift in consumer preferences weaker. But Wicksell argued that this was only a temporary blessing, because as the population kept growing, the structure of the New World economy would gradually approximate that of the Old World.

The next parameter shift to be discussed is one mentioned more *en passant* by Wicksell (see Chapter 4): capital movements. We have to compare the effects of a growth of capital stocks in the Old World with the growth of those of the New World, assuming that capitalists are free to decide where they want accumulation to take place. We then want to focus on the development of the two wage rates. Let us start in the Old World. Again we differentiate (8.3)–(8.5) at constant commodity prices and with a given labor force. The exogenous change is the increase in K_{OA} and K_{OM}.

Differentiating the system and solving for the change in the wage rate yields:

$$dw_O = -(1/\Delta)P(A_O^{LK}M_O^{LL}dK_{OA} + M_O^{LK}A_O^{LL}dK_{OM}) > 0 \qquad (8.67)$$

Regardless of which of the two capital stocks (probably both) that grows, the wage rate will increase. Whether labor will move from manufacturing to agriculture or vice versa depends on the differences in capital accumulation on the one hand and on the impact of additional capital on the marginal productivities of labor on the other:

$$dL_{OA} = -dL_{OM} = (1/\Delta)(PA_O^{LK}dK_{OA} - M_O^{LK}dK_{OM}) \qquad (8.68)$$

Wicksell implicitly compared (8.67) and (8.68) with the analogous expressions for capital accumulation in the New World, arguing that from the point of view of the prospective emigrants capital formation overseas would be preferable, i.e. for $dK_{NA} = dK_{OA}$ and $dK_{NM} = dK_{OM}$, $A_N^{LK} > A_O^{LK}$ and $M_N^{LK} > M_O^{LK}$.

The only parameter change in the Wicksellian system that we have not investigated so far is war (Chapter 5). As we know, Wicksell was constantly worried that overpopulation would result in territorial aggression. How can this be handled in the model? If we stick to the sequence that Wicksell obviously had in mind, war is triggered by population growth, and the short-run effect of war is a reduction of the population of the nations involved in the war, both as a result of the belligerent activities *per se* and as a result of starvation, etc. that follows in the footsteps of war. This, then, would reverse all sequences that we have already dealt with that are triggered by population growth. However, according to Wicksell, war 'solves' the population problem only in the short run, because at some point after the termination of the war activities there will again be a drive to increase the population, possibly triggered by the rulers, politicians and militaries of the countries that have suffered, and then we are of course back where we began our analysis in this chapter.

The present chapter has been devoted to the exercise of putting all the bits and pieces of Wicksell's scattered analysis of population growth together. The result is astonishing. Far from confirming the conventional wisdom that what he wrote on the population question was mechanical and simplistic, it turns out that the exercise results in a coherent general equilibrium framework that very much resembles the specific factors model of international trade developed by Ronald Jones (and Paul Samuelson) in 1971. Within this setting, Wicksell handled factor growth (population, natural resources, capital), technological progress, tariffs, and factor movements. In this, he stands out as a precursor of the modern theory of international trade. It is here then, rather than in the use of the optimum population concept, that Wicksell's original contribution to the analysis of population growth lies.

9 Why was Wicksell accused of lack of originality?

Given the originality of mind that was one of Wicksell's hallmarks, and given our findings in Chapter 8, there is an inevitable question that must be raised: Why has Wicksell been accused of not producing anything very original when it comes to poverty, population, and emigration? (The only exception made is his writings on the concept of optimal population, but this, as we know, he never really developed.) The only possible answers to our question are conjectural but, even so, it may be worthwhile to speculate on the issue.

Too early

One reason may be that Wicksell discovered the population problem very early in his career. At the time when he delivered his scandalous lecture at *Hoppets Här* he had not yet been exposed to any formal study of economics. On the contrary, he entered the debate as an amateur who had had a revelation. He had seen the neo-Malthusian light in Drysdale's book and he would spend the rest of life arguing that the population question was the most important of all the social questions. His basic views on poverty, population and emigration were formed already in 1880–1, i.e. extremely early in his academic career – at a time when the only thing that he had published within his main field at the time was six mathematical notes in a pedagogical journal directed to students (Knudtzon, 1976: 82).

The basic causal order in Wicksell's early system was simple. Excessive population growth led to poverty, and poverty produced drunkenness and prostitution on the one hand and emigration to an uncertain existence on the other. Emigration was not an unmitigated blessing. Far from that. It entailed a loss of human capital for the country that the emigrants left, to be set against the cost of the formation of this capital. The remedy was simple as well. The sexual instincts had to be taken for granted but, if contraceptive devices could be made available and the population could be enlightened with respect to their use, the incidence of drunkenness and prostitution would be reduced. People would stay home enjoying safe sex within the family, and the economy – always subject to diminishing returns – would be able to absorb the increase in the labor force without any need for emigration. With time, Wicksell would develop this core argument into the refined architecture involving international trade that we met in Chapter 8.

After the lecture at *Hoppets Här* and the publication of Wicksell's (1999a) pamphlet, David Davidson, as we found in Chapter 2, accused him of not having studied enough economics. This, Wicksell admitted, was true, but it was of completely subordinate importance. The important thing was that he had his arguments in good order. It was the *arguments* that Davidson had to refute. 'If he cannot do that, it is really irrelevant how much or how little I had studied before forming my opinions' (Gårdlund, 1996: 60), Wicksell replied. He was of course right, and he was also irritated that Davidson through his critique had chosen to play into the hands of the more violent critics. But it could not be helped that Wicksell would rapidly be branded by his detractors as a radical amateur without adequate theoretical preparation for the task he had set out to deal with. Carl Uhr (1951: 10–11) provides a succinct summary:

> Had it not been for the fact that the substance of his lecture was reported in the daily press, Wicksell might calmly have returned to his mathematical studies. But as it was, what he had to say reached a wider, more articulate public. Since it offended against the mores of the times just as the Darwinian theory of evolution in an earlier day offended against theological dogma, the response was immediate and strong. He was criticized and reviled in the press by professors of medicine, clergymen, essayists, and editors. Overnight he achieved the unenviable reputation of a 'moral nihilist' and came to be regarded as the leader of a suspect small intellectual sect known as – neo-Malthusians. He defended himself ably and with courage in articles and tracts, all of which added to his notoriety.

A religion

One reason that may have made latter-day students of Wicksell's works on population argue that these were less than original is that his views were formed in an atmosphere of almost religious ecstasy. As an adolescent, Wicksell had displayed a deep religious conviction. His early childhood appears to have been very happy, with a generally joyful mood prevailing in the family. His mother Christina, however, died of tuberculosis in 1858, when Knut was only six years old. A few years later his father, Johan, remarried a woman who was not exceedingly fond of his children, and Knut was left in an emotional vacuum. In 1866, Johan Wicksell passed away as well, with cancer. Knut was fifteen and orphaned. Relatives had to step in and care for Johan's and Christina's five children. Under these circumstances, it hardly comes as a surprise to learn that young Knut rapidly turned to religion (Swedberg, 1998: 109), and religion for him became a serious matter. As he described it himself (quoted in Gårdlund, 1996: 25):

> I could hold up my head no longer. Sin became my daily companion and when for the first time I came under the influence of a truly religious person when I was prepared for confirmation, my self-reliance broke down. It was a deeply repentant, dreadfully guilt-laden sinner of just over fifteen, who crept up to the communion table on Palm Sunday 1867 to beg for a share in the virtue of Christ.

The intensity of Wicksell's religious conviction continued to rise until 1870 when he arrived at what Gårdlund (1996: 25) qualifies as a 'total conversion.' The trigger was almost bizarre (Gårdlund, 1996: 25):

> . . . he thought that Sweden would be drawn into the Franco-Prussian War and realized that he would not dare to go there and fight for fear of being killed and going to Hell as a sinner. From that moment he devoted the whole of his time to repentance. He began to read the Bible daily and became a regular church-goer. 'The Bible was no longer to lie hidden obscurely in a dusty corner of the bookcase, it was to be my daily reading and, furthermore, it must be left out on my table as proof that at least one man was not ashamed of the Gospel of Christ.'

Wicksell's religious problems would soon develop into what may be described as a crisis. He rejected reading fiction, going to the theater (which before had been his favorite pastime) and going to cafés, because of the presence of female waitresses (Gårdlund, 1996: 30). In the end, the crisis provoked a rejection of religion and turned Wicksell into a convinced anticlerical. This took place in the spring of 1874. He had gradually been convinced that a conflict existed between faith and science and the more he had read to the contrary the more convinced he became. 'There is no surer method of eradicating the last remnants of faith than by reading bad apologies for it, and in my experience most of them are bad' (quoted in Gårdlund, 1996: 31–2).

Wicksell would demonstrate his new, anticlerical, stance regularly during the rest of his life, challenging the dogmas of the church. His position culminated in a lecture delivered on 2 November 1908 before a Socialist audience in Stockholm. There he referred to the 'altar' as the symbol of religious intolerance. 'It implies, as it were, an entailed estate of about 15 million kronor each year in all our wallets and in addition a servitude on the education of all our children' (Wicksell, 1909: 27–8). Even more defiant was the passage that rendered him two months in jail in Ystad for blasphemy (Gårdlund, 1996: 249):

> What are we to say about this tale of the Holy Ghost and the Virgin Mary? Well, we cannot say that he exactly seduced the girl, she was certainly willing enough; at first invitation she curtsied [apparently at this point, on the platform, the little plump Wicksell dropped a curtsy] and said: 'Behold the handmaid of the Lord.' without even asking her betrothed. We cannot help feeling sorry for the poor man; what had he done to deserve being placed in such a predicament? [. . .] I am almost sure that, for all his piety, he would grumble a little to himself about what had happened and perhaps, when no-one was listening, would ask in his secret heart: 'Why the devil couldn't the Holy Ghost let me make my little Jesus myself?'

Wicksell's speech was later published as a pamphlet (Wicksell, 1909), however, without the quoted passage, which was what rendered him the two months.[1]

That Wicksell had turned away from official religion, however, did not mean that he went through life without guidelines. On the contrary, as Rolf Henriksson (1991: 40) has observed,

> . . . the fact was that Wicksell remained as religious as he ever had been. He had just changed religion. In turning his interests and attention towards social issues he met with a new faith in Neomalthusianism. This utilitarian reformism became then his commitment for life. He published pamphlets and papers on neomalthusian issues in an ongoing campaign from the early 1880s until his death in 1926, seemingly without faltering from this second confession of his.

Wicksell himself came close to describing his 'conversion' in the same terms. In an autobiographical sketch, written at the age of forty (Wicksell, 1890b), he described how he left:

> . . . a state of mind [which] often bordered on deep depression, as I regarded both my own life and existence in general as failures.

It was only the work of Malthus or actually the excerpt thereof that

that is found in the well-known book The Elements of Social Science, published in Swedish translation for the first time in 1878, that shed light for me on all these questions; and when at the beginning of 1880 by chance I happened to publicly defend the neo-Malthusian doctrine myself and then experienced what a mass of inherited prejudice that remain to be exterminated in precisely this field that I also felt that I had received something to live for myself.

Gårdlund agrees. Taking stock of Wicksell's intellectual and emotional development in the 1880s, he concludes (Gårdlund, 1996: 73):

The last few years had seen important developments in Wicksell's life. Neo-Malthusianism had brought him a new faith and stimulated his interest in the scientific study of social questions. On the other hand his public lectures and the subsequent notoriety had interrupted his career as a natural scientist. For at least ten years to come he was to be torn between a longing for the scientific career he had originally chosen and a growing desire to devote himself to the study and propagation of neo-Malthusianism. It was not until the 1890's that he recognized theoretical economics as a field giving scope to both these impulses.

Out of place

Wicksell's quasi-religious conviction in population matters inevitably meant that his neo-Malthusianism had a tendency to show up in all kinds of situations, also when not called for at all, and hence contribute to the view that it was loosely founded and mechanical. Thus, in a letter to his friend Öhrvall, dated 11 July 1882 (Hashimoto, 1996: 59), when Wicksell was on summer holiday in the countryside near Vimmerby in eastern Småland, staying with his sister and brother-in-law, he describes the local situation:

Malthusian ideas are not adhered to here to any large extent. The parish school teacher, for example, has 9 living children, what seems rather clever when you have an occupation that is remunerated with 600 kronor per annum, cow food as well as a free two-room apartment and free firewood. However, he is supposed to make some little extra income on the one hand (I think), as an organist, and on the other hand by leasing a small farm, but the consequence of this is that the school is run accordingly. The farmers as well have very numerous families, but in spite of this the population of the parish hardly increases at all, but the neighboring areas, the cities and the United States of North

America are blessed with the surplus. Here is thus a complete 'vagina gentium.'

Another recurrent occasion was in Wicksell's teaching and tutoring of students both in Uppsala and in Lund, where he finally got a chair in Political Economy and Fiscal Law in 1901, but only after a scandalous prelude, caused, of course, by his radical views of social problems.[2] For his students, acceptance of the neo-Malthusian doctrine was close to compulsory (Gårdlund, 1996: 216–17):

> The neo-Malthusian flavour of his lectures and his criticism of socialist theory made a great impression on many of his students, but for those with an independent interest in the higher study of science he was probably not a particularly good teacher. His own ideas were so deeply rooted that he was not very successful at helping other people to develop theirs. Practically all students requesting an essay subject in economics were told to write on Malthusianism. Anyone who did not accept Malthus was never wholly accepted by Wicksell. His passionate[3] attitude on this point is revealed by the intimidating words he once used to his younger colleague Gustaf Steffen, who as yet had no definite appointment and whose views on the population question did not agree with his own. He exhorted Steffen to revise his outlook as soon as possible, 'otherwise I shall certainly have to submit you to special treatment, for an economist who is not completely saturated in Malthus is like a sailing ship without rudder, compass or ballast.'

In his obituary of his teacher, Emil Sommarin (1926–7: 25–6) stresses Wicksell's tendency to bring out his neo-Malthusian viewpoints under the least expected circumstances:

> With a disposition for sharpening his statements, possibly reinforced by having experienced the difficulty of getting attention for viewpoints that people stubbornly persisted in not wanting to take into account – a stubbornness that drove the otherwise considerate man to tell the plain truth on occasions and under circumstances where his behavior would have maximum shock impact – . . . [Wicksell] sharpened his warnings against continued population growth to statements regarding the necessity of a strong population decline because of the long-standing overexploitation of the natural resources of the country, and above all of its forests.

Out of fashion

A fourth reason for the scepticism with which Wicksell's writings on population have been viewed, may be that Malthusianism simply had gone out of fashion at the time when he began his writings on poverty and population. There were not many people supporting Wicksell in the public debate. Schumpeter (1954: 581–2) points out that during the course of the nineteenth century the Malthusian theory of population 'just as free trade had become the "right" policy, which only ignorance or obliquity could possibly fail to accept – part and parcel of the eternal truth that had been observed once and for all.' Richard Goodwin (1979: 191) makes the same point:

> Thus economics became in the early nineteenth century the dismal science because it predicted a homeostatic feed-back mechanism for the standard of living: no matter how much technology progresses, the population would increase and swamp the increased product. In the long run the level of consumption had always to be at that level which equated births and deaths.

However, Schumpeter also notes that after 1850 the interest in population questions among professional economists faded. The neoclassics 'rarely failed to pay their respects to the shibboleth,' with one significant exception: 'At the end of the century the one leading man to take . . . [the population question] seriously was Wicksell, who also resuscitated the doctrine of optimal population which, however, had commanded support throughout' (Schumpeter, 1954: 582).

Even so, before World War I, it was mainly from his fellow convinced neo-Malthusians that Wicksell received appreciation for his views. Only later things would change, and Wicksell would receive at least some of his due (Gårdlund, 1996: 320):

> Immediately before the war . . . [Wicksell] had been made Vice President of the international neo-Malthusian organization. Some years later he was granted the small triumph of having one of England's foremost economists give a neo-Malthusian interpretation of the German expansion. 'Until now Edgeworth was almost anti-Malthusian,' he wrote to Öhrvall, 'I tried to push him towards Malthusianism (in his early days); it seems to have had some success.'

After the war, neo-Malthusianism made a comeback in England. During the Fifth International Neo-Malthusian and Birth Control Conference, celebrated in London under the auspices of the Malthusian League in 1922, the economic and statistical section was chaired by Keynes, 'who, on the occasion of a visit to Malthus' home, propounded the advanced views [in the population question] which were later to appear in his articles and books' (Gårdlund, 1990: 349; 1996: 320).

The Swedish attitude

The cold international attitude toward neo-Malthusianism was echoed in Sweden. Gårdlund (1996: 346-47) relates how only two of Wicksell's younger colleagues showed an understanding of his position:

> There was little support for Wicksell's views on population in economic circles where, on other subjects, he was regarded as an authority. [Excepting Emil Sommarin it seems only to have been Sven Brisman, who had been a radical ever since his student years in Gothenburg, who in this question was on Wicksell's side (Gårdlund, 1990: 346).][4] Since to him these views were a living faith, Wicksell was deeply grieved by the lack of appreciation. On one occasion, in 1923, when he was criticized by Eli Heckscher at a meeting of the Economists' Club, he sat down afterwards and wrote a sorrowful letter on the subject. The letter was never sent . . .

Not even Sommarin, his successor at Lund, appears to have been completely convinced. In his autobiography he relates how during an oral examination for Wicksell everything went fine – with one exception: population (Sommarin, 1947: 141):

> Long afterwards Wicksell during a public debate remarked that it had always been 'a thorn in the flesh' for him that he had failed to convert me to his viewpoint in the population question. There was, however, no difference between us as far as population theory was concerned, but to take part in the neo-Malthusian propaganda; for that I found no reason [. . .] the two-child system had to lead to a declining population, which I found economically dubious, especially if the target was put as low as 3 million, which Wicksell did. If a population decline had set in – of this I was convinced – it would probably turn out to be difficult to stop it and stabilize the population or to make it grow again to the desired level. This was disputed by Wicksell . . .

We have already (in Chapter 2) met the violent initial reaction in Sweden against Wicksell's views on the population question. This criticism was not to recede for quite some time to come. The Swedish intellectual climate prevailing at the time was one of simple narrow-mindedness, bigotry, and what would today be labeled 'political correctness.' As late as 1919 he was criticized vehemently by a younger Swedish economist, Nils Wohlin (Gårdlund, 1996: 319):

> At a famous *Verdandi*[5] meeting in February 1919, Nils Wohlin ... launched a vigorous attack 'before it is too late' on Wicksell's 'propaganda, in the guise of science, for the ruin of Sweden.' Wohlin pointed out that industrial development had emphatically contradicted the frequent neo-Malthusian prophesies of ruin. The idea that there would be a diminishing return from industry, if the population continued to grow, was based on the unrealistic assumption that technical development had come to a standstill.
>
> The greater part of Wohlin's criticism, however, consisted of eloquent moralizing. Any decline in fertility would be 'appalling'; if families were limited to two children each, this would have a 'detrimental effect on enterprise and spiritual strength' and finally neo-Malthusianism was a 'rotting fungus in the garden of our emotions.'

Of course, Wicksell was hailed and supported by young radicals and by the growing labor movement. Ernst Wigforss, Finance Minister 1925–6 and 1932–49, and also the leading social democratic theoretician, recalls in his autobiography the impression that Wicksell made on him during his early days as a student and academic in Lund (Wigforss, 1950: 189):

> His complete freedom from considerations of what could be useful or pleasant for himself, his unyielding desire to tell the truth as he saw it, and to say things which usually were unpleasant for the mighty, the powerful and the prevailing opinions, all this was likely to make young people with critical views of society stand guard around him even when they did not share his opinions. It was not a blind devotion for something resembling martyrdom. When you could later, yourself, speak in front of large gatherings and get applauses during meetings you were not ignorant about the fact that you can have a fair amount of success defying a dominant opinion when you are backed by your own, possibly growing, opinion. That Wicksell gathered strength from the support of such circles, that, from his earliest battles, he had got used to the pleasure of always being by far the most extreme, and that he appreciated it, all this we could ponder and yet tell ourselves that it was good that such natures can be born and work like a salt among the humans.

Standing alone

Yet, as it turned out, Wicksell stood pretty much alone. The support from the labor movement was not unconditional. Wigforss (1950: 189–90) stresses that 'he never concealed those of his opinions that the labor movement disliked' and that the support came from 'rather wide circles' in it, but Wicksell was never an organized social democrat. In his memoirs, Tage Erlander, Swedish Prime Minister 1946–69, recalls a meeting with Wicksell during his student days in Lund, which produced a revealing statement (Erlander, 1972: 122):

> Wicksell counted as a Social Democrat. However, he never belonged to the party. In spite of this he was invited to talk at the 25th anniversary of the local party body [*arbetarekommun*] of Lund in 1926. He expressed his pleasure of having been invited as keynote speaker for the celebration but added: 'I do not belong to the flock. I am a sheep on my own.'

Richard Swedberg (1999: 519) has argued that the support for Wicksell was stronger that what is commonly realized:

> . . . the case of Wicksell make[s] us realize that acts of civil courage are always embedded in a social context and that Wicksell had quite a bit of social support for his oppositional activities. Wicksell, for example, often defended causes that were part of larger social movements in Sweden. His advocacy of temperance as well as birth control and the freedom of speech are examples of this. Wicksell, as we know, was able to support himself for several years in the 1890s by traveling around the country as a public speaker. Later on in his career, Wicksell was also sheltered by the tradition at Swedish universities not to let a person's political opinions stand in the way for him or her being appointed to a professorship – or being dismissed, once appointed to such a professorship. Wicksell had furthermore throughout his adult life not only a network of acquaintances and sympathizers to draw on, but also two extremely close friends (Theodor Frölander and Hjalmar Öhrvall), who always backed him up, morally as well as with money. The strong support from his wife (whom he married in 1899) must also be mentioned in this context. And last but not least, Wicksell had from early on immersed himself in the tradition of 'the religion of humanity' (Durkheim), in which he found moral support for many of his ideas.

Swedberg's observation may be correct, but the support that Wicksell undoubtedly had in some circles must be put against the resistance of the dominant opinion. The three examples cited by Swedberg himself are eloquent illustrations of this: the speech at *Hoppets Här* in 1980, which rendered Wicksell an admonition from Uppsala University, a speech he gave in Lund in 1905, after the dissolution of the union between Sweden and Norway, which he was prevented from finishing, and the 1908 speech that rendered him two months in jail for blasphemy. As we have seen, spreading his message during lecture tours at times was close to impossible, and Wicksell received his professorship only after a long, protracted and unfair battle against him.

It is impossible that all this would not have made a deep impression on Wicksell. In a talk on the population issue in the Scandinavian countries delivered on 11 February 1891, he (Wicksell, 1891a: 216) complained: 'The undersigned has been the only one talking about the evils of overpopulation during the past 11 years.' Obviously, he felt that his neo-Malthusian mission was very much a one-man crusade, but given Wicksell's well-known stubbornness (Henriksson, 1991: 39), it is quite possible that this simply reinforced his determination to win, and by the same token cemented his views and made them impossible to change, other than when it came to details. In a letter to Erik Lindahl, dated 14 January 1952, Britta Collinder, the granddaughter of Knut Wicksell's sister, adds some more personality traits (Hashimoto, 1995: 297):

> Uncle Knut's social pathos was probably due on the one hand to his habit of having a deviant point of view, on the other hand on never having been afraid, and as far as I understand he did not understand what it meant to be afraid. Nor did my grandmother. It is an almost pathological lack in the spiritual equipment of that family. They are not afraid and their internal fights have always taken place on the theoretical level.

These personality traits were shared by Wicksell's fellow radical combatants elsewhere. Gårdlund summarizes (1990: 364):[6]

> Many of Wicksell's most salient characteristics also appear among the great radicals in other countries. It appears likely that people with similar qualities – rationality, independence and courage – were gathering to the battle against the authoritarian society that was being waged in many places, and their similarity probably increased because during the battle years they lived under the sway of the same doctrine and under the same difficult circumstances.

Wicksell was what his friend Theodor Frölander termed a 'lone confessor' with 'a little religion of his own' (quoted by Gårdlund, 1990: 373), and he was himself the first person to admit this.

One-man crusades rest on conviction and little else, and conviction Wicksell certainly had. In one of his unpublished articles dealing with the German reparation problem he wrote: 'The population question, this most sovereign of all social issues will, if I am not mistaken, find its final solution during the present century, and the future will honor those peoples who have then been in the vanguard' (Wicksell, 1923: 205).

This, Wicksell's detractors have interpreted as dogmatism. But to argue that Wicksell's conviction amounted to dogmatism is going too far. Rather, as Richard Swedberg (1999) has stressed, Wicksell was a prime example of *civil courage*, of the courage to act because of your conviction even although the price for this may be high. 'Of course,' Gårdlund (1990: 373) argues, he was a lone confessor '. . . although this fanatical trait receded toward the end of his life and had not even earlier made its appearance other than in flashes in a work which on the whole was stamped by reason and reflection.' It was usually not Wicksell who lost his temper, but his adversaries who acted 'wildly and without restraint' (Gårdlund, 1990: 366). Dogmatism is one thing, conviction another. To a large extent it was the format that Wicksell chose for his presentations – pamphlets, speeches and public lectures under all kinds of possible, and frequently also impossible, circumstances, which regularly served to bring him into trouble – that made his views appear as dogmatic and not original. During the furious disputes that preceded his appointment as professor in Lund, one of his adversaries held out his 'pernicious, unpatriotic activities as an enlightener of the people,' and another claimed that promoting Wicksell to the position of professor would give 'a semblance of improper encouragement to the narrow, fanatical and subversive activities of a closet-scholar' (Gårdlund, 1996: 219).

The failure of the critics

The critics failed to see the originality of Wicksell's approach. Even disregarding the arguments presented so far, this is understandable. In 1891, when they first appeared in an elaborated version, the modern theory of international trade and factor movements had not yet been worked out. Eli Heckscher had not yet written his path-breaking article. This would not appear until 1919 (Heckscher, 1991), Bertil Ohlin's dissertation (Ohlin, 1991) was defended in 1924, his big treatise on international trade was published only in 1933 (Ohlin, 1933), Paul Samuelson's (1939; 1948; 1949; 1953; also Stolper and Samuelson, 1941) contributions came only around World War II, and the specific factors model was not formalized until 1971.

It is thus no wonder that Wicksell failed to spell out his model explicitly. Such was the state of the arts when he wrote, and he should of course not be blamed for that.

Wicksell's complete views on population and poverty have to be put together from a large number of scattered sources. Once this is done, however, the result is astonishing: a general equilibrium system based on the specific factors approach: something that would not be completely developed until some eighty years after the appearance of the long essay in French on population, although Gottfried Haberler (1936) had begun to explore it in the 1930s, a contribution which, however, went largely unnoticed (Maneschi, 1998: 162–7). It was the analysis of how the interaction between population growth and diminishing returns drove people out of Europe during the late nineteenth century that Wicksell was concerned with, and in the process he inadvertently became a precursor of modern trade and factor movement theory. No neoclassical economist working within the factor proportions framework today would have treated the problem of population growth and poverty very differently.

Like Malthus and Ricardo, Wicksell failed to foresee the direction that technological change would take. He did not predict the rapid industrial development of the twentieth century. In the Swedish case, he missed the 'genius industries': the branches that built on some original invention (Swedberg, 1998: 47, note). That is understandable and it must, of course, be taken into consideration when we read Wicksell's works today. But who can predict the future? That is completely beside the point. Besides, Wicksell is in excellent company (Uhr, 1962: 337):

> ... his remarkable foresight and analytical powers notwithstanding, Wicksell underestimated some of his own country's growth potential, chiefly in the technological realm as it affects productivity and industrial diversification. In this he shares the fate of many who have attempted to peer into the distant future. It is clear that while he was not an infallible prophet, he was much more foresighted about the shape of things to come, and much less wrong, than some of his distinguished contemporaries, notably, Walras, Pareto, and Alfred Marshall.

What Wicksell cannot be accused of is to have failed to provide a formulation of his ideas on population growth, poverty and emigration that was both consistent and original. Wicksell's writings are no mere carbon copies of those of Malthus. From at least 1891 he developed his own analysis and he is remarkably 'modern' in his treatment.

Wicksell also differed from Malthus in his moral position. During the Malthusian League conference in London in 1922, Wicksell posed the problem of why the Malthusian doctrine had not met with more practical success (Hashimoto, forthcoming, Letter 176): 'There has always been some uncertainty about the real meaning of the Malthusian doctrine, and this, no doubt, depends on some faults in the doctrine itself, grand and all-important as it may be in the general effect.' Wicksell summarized the message contained in the first edition of Malthus' *Essay on the Principle of Population* ('quite another work than the later editions') by pointing out that 'under happy circumstances,' i.e. a sufficient supply of foodstuffs, a people would double its numbers every twenty-five years, but as these circumstances do not exist, no nation can ever be happy and the majority must be wretched. 'In the last two chapters he then tries to console us for this rather gloomy view, saying that people really have no business being happy on earth, but only to prepare themselves for the future state.'

In the subsequent editions, said Wicksell, Malthus tried to mitigate his views by allowing for the possibility of moral restraint, 'late marriage and chastity in the single state – as a way of checking population without misery or vice.' However, 'the amelioration was not a very essential one, because Malthus himself did not believe much in the effectiveness of that moral restraint.' Next, Wicksell went on to point to Malthus' polemic with Arthur Young in 1806, reprinted in the appendix to the second edition of the *Essay* (Malthus, 1989, Vol. II: 221):

> Mr. Young has asserted that I have made perfect chastity in the single state absolutely necessary to the success of my plan; but this surely is a misrepresentation . . . I have said . . . that it is our duty to defer marriage till we can feed our children, and that it is also our duty not to indulge ourselves in vicious gratifications; but I have never said that I expected either, much less both, of these duties to be completely fulfilled. In this, and a number of other cases, it may happen that the violation of one of two duties will enable a man to perform the other with greater facility; but if they really be both duties and both practicable, no power *on earth* can absolve a man from the guilt of violating either. This can be done only by that God who can weigh the crime against the temptation, and will temper justice with mercy.

Wicksell was indignant, and argued that Malthus' reasoning led him to the a contradiction that was instrumental when it came to making his message fall on barren ground (Hashimoto, forthcoming, Letter 176):

> It would be easy, of course, to drive those reflections of Malthus into absurdity. If indeed, God, according to Malthus, is likely to be rather indulgent towards the unchastity in the single state, why should He be

so very particular about the use of contraceptives in the matrimonial state? Even there the temptation is very great indeed. Why should not God in this case 'weigh the crime against the temptation' and be willing to 'temper justice with mercy'?

Of course it is preposterous to place a question of the greatest social bearing solely under the narrow aspect of ecclesiastical morals. If there were no other objection to a loose sexual life than God, a *modus vivendi* might perhaps be got at. Unfortunately there are other consequences, the scourge of venereal disease, the unspeakable abjectness of the phenomena of prostitution and so forth. But on those things Malthus does not speak a word.

To my mind this half-heartedness of Malthus has been the great hindrance of the success of his doctrine.

Wicksell refutes the doctrine of Malthus because its roots are found in the conventional religious teachings.

In summary, what seems to have misled the critics is the almost religious conviction with which Wicksell presented his views. It was easy to see him as a mere social agitator as soon as the population issue came up, and much of what he wrote was published in popular pamphlets intended to have a practical impact – pamphlets that appear obscure today. Knut Wicksell wanted to 'educate the Swedish people' (Gårdlund, 1996: 305).[7] Hence all the pamphlets and lectures. The more substantial French prize essay, in turn, appears to have been read by less than a handful of people, at least during the past fifty or sixty years. Wicksell's 'scientific contributions' were published in books and journals, i.e. in the form accepted by his contemporary and latter-day colleagues. This should, however, not obscure the fact that once we start putting all Wicksell's scattered writings on population and poverty together, without regard for under what circumstances and in what form they were published, we find that they do indeed form a coherent body of thought, within a framework that would await its formal modeling for eight decades. In the end Wicksell's originality extended into his analysis of poverty and population as well.

In fact, it can be argued that the analysis has stood the test of time better than the problem that called for it. In 1934, eight years after Wicksell's death, Gunnar and Alva Myrdal published a book on the population issue in Sweden that would serve as the programmatic publication for the emerging welfare state (Myrdal and Myrdal, 1935). By the time their work was published, the growth of the Swedish population had been reduced to the point where the two Myrdals feared that its size would begin to shrink, and their main concern was that this would place a heavy burden on a shrinking share in working age to care for the increasing share of elderly people. With respect to the neo-Malthusian movement in Sweden they had the following to say (Myrdal and Myrdal, 1935: 63):

> . . . neo-Malthusianism stands victorious on its last line of battle. The movement has thus reached the end of the tether and seen its demands realized. Nobody will in the future question that children should be born only as a result of the free choice of their parents. The neo-Malthusian movement then in the case of Sweden belongs to history. It is entitled to its monument, but in positive terms it has nothing more to offer.

The Myrdals offer their own tribute (Myrdal and Myrdal, 1935: 113–14):

> The neo-Malthusians in the eighties and at the turn of the century [. . .] were in a situation where they saw people live miserably and bear unreasonably large batches of children and where annually tens of thousands were driven to emigrate. Facing this situation they were driven to advocate birth control. That this view of population policy was compassionate and correct is now realized by people deeply within the conservative camp. The old neo-Malthusians finally receive the belated rehabilitation after fierce and sometimes sordid persecution that their theses are being cautiously accepted by conservative clergymen, journalists and moralists, or in any case by the large inarticulate upper or middle class opinion that previously resisted them bitterly.

First and foremost among the neo-Malthusians was Wicksell. The Myrdals (1935: 37–48) offer an extensive account of his 1880 temperance lodge speech and the criticism he received. They conclude (Myrdal and Myrdal, 1935, 47–8):

> This entire discussion, which is so close to us in time, now gives a grotesque impression. Precisely therefore it has an educational value for us to have to face the opinions that existed at the time in unembellished form. We have something important to learn from them. Our time as well is full of prejudice and false pathos, our notions of the external social world are obscure and our moral and political positions will therefore appear as grotesque in the eyes of a near future.

This was one of Wicksell's major contributions to the Swedish debate. In a stuffy, narrow-minded and sometimes outright stupid era he 'opened' the debate climate, and he scored some important victories. Torsten Gårdlund (1990: 373) summarizes:

Of the social reforms that he had struggled for – extended suffrage, social and economic equalization within a by and large preserved market system, equality for women, increased freedom of opinion, admission of birth control, increased concertation in the labor market, socially oriented industrial policy – many had been carried out during his own time and others were well on their way at the time of his death.

Eli Heckscher (1921) paid his tribute to Wicksell's steadfastness on the occasion of Wicksell's seventieth birthday:

> . . . there is perhaps no person in modern Sweden who, as much as he, has understood to live his life in accordance with his own being . . . and follow his thought to its end, state his opinion, and live his life without regard for dangers, be they intellectual or moral, social or individual. And for nothing does he deserve to be thanked as much as for this.[8]

'Wicksell had the integrity of a saint,' writes Gunnar Myrdal. 'Few people have walked through life as untouched by moral compromises as he' (Myrdal, 1972: 271). These qualities he used in the public debate, driven by what he thought was fair and just (Jonung, 2001: 47). Wicksell was indomitable. He 'gathered a generation around the demand for an open debate of social issues' (Gårdlund, 1990: 361). He did it not least in his work on the population question: in his speeches and public scandals, and in his pamphlets. This for Wicksell was an issue of such dignity that his duty 'to educate the Swedish people' took over completely, pushing his scientific thinking on the issue into the background. As Erik Lindahl (1958: 44) has reminded us:

> His time and energy sufficed both for the furthering of science and for the participation in the work of removing the anomalies existing in society. [. . .] For him, therefore, scientific work was not an interesting game of theoretical trickery – although he certainly derived intellectual satisfaction from it – but was justified as a means of furthering our knowledge of the possibilities of increasing general well-being.

All the time, however, what Wicksell did in the public sphere had a solid foundation in his scientific thinking, and, despite what has been alleged, this is the case also with his views of population growth and poverty. Hopefully the present work, offered in the spirit of Knut Wicksell himself, can contribute to rectify, or at least add to, the conventional picture of his contribution.

Plate 3 Mats Lundahl at Ystad.

Plate 4 Mats Lundahl at Ystad (note the prison rules on the wall beside him).

Notes

1 Introduction

1 See, however, Boianovsky (2001: 142, note 17).
2 See also the list in Hashimoto (2001).
3 Emphasis added.

2 Tumultuous beginnings: the cause of poverty and its remedy

1 Gårdlund (1996: 46) reports that it is impossible to discover who translated Drysdale's book into Swedish. This issue does not appear in half a century of correspondence between Wicksell and Öhrvall. Hence they would not know (Gårdlund, 1990: 380).
2 Wicksell's own translation reads 'Some words about the principal causes and remedies of social evils intemperance especially noticed' (Hashimoto, 1996: 34).
3 Myrdal and Myrdal (1935: 37–48) provides a good summary of the criticism.
4 For information about Davidson, see Uhr (1975; 1991b).
5 Boströmianism was a specific, original, Swedish school, founded by Christopher Jacob Boström (1797–1866), which dominated the philosophical scene in the country during the later half of the nineteenth century. The school contended that to every human being on earth corresponded an eternal idea in a hierarchy with God at the top, encompassing all these ideas. It was politically conservative but radical in religious matters. Boströmianism gradually died out after the turn of the century. For an account, see Nordin (1981).
6 This passage is not included in the English translation in Gårdlund (1996).
7 Wicksell (1882).

3 The causes of population growth: the French prize essay

1 This essay only exists in a version written by hand by Wicksell's wife, Anna Bugge, which is the version of the *Académie des sciences morales et politiques de l'Institut de France*. A draft version in Wicksell's own handwriting is in the Wicksell archive at the University Library at Lund University. I am indebted to Hitoshi Hashimoto, who, with Michel Robine, is in the process of editing Wicksell's prize essay for publication, for generously providing me with a transcription of this document.

106 *Notes*

2 Sommarin (1926–7: 21) reports that when Wicksell had retired from his chair in Lund and moved to a new-built house in Mörby, north of Stockholm, he ' [o]nly half jokingly . . . found the danger of being rusticated in this not exactly rural suburb worrying . . .'
3 Here (not in 1893 and 1901, respectively – cf. Boianovsky 2001: 130) is where Wicksell sets down his ideas about optimum population and introduces the term for the first time in his writings.
4 Cf. the Domar (1970) thesis on the causes of slavery: In a situation where you have free workers and free land you cannot simultaneously have a non-working upper class.
5 Wicksell did not win the *Prix Rossi*, but he received a 'consolation prize' of 500 francs as well as encouraging comments from the French economist Émile Levasseur who was the one reporting on the competition and its outcome (Gårdlund, 1996: 150).

4 The centerpiece of Wicksell's theory: diminishing returns

1 An analytical treatment of this is offered in Coleman (1985).
2 The origin of this discussion is probably to be found in the fact that Wicksell had read Ricardo's (1971) famous chapter 'On Machinery' in the third edition of the *Principles*. There Ricardo claimed that labor-saving innovations in agriculture could produce unemployment, because they would make the total product fall, while simultaneously increasing the net revenue, i.e. the part accruing as rent to the landowners in agriculture. Wicksell (1934: 133–44; 1958b: 100–6; 1981) refuted Ricardo, arguing that the wage rate would fall and hence make for a reabsorption of the workers, and besides that the total product must increase. For a nice exposition of the former argument, see Hansson (1983). See also the introduction to Wicksell (1981), by Jonung (1981) as well as Samuelson (1989).

5 Overpopulation, specialization, and trade

1 The official correspondence is reprinted as an appendix to Wicksell (1887a).
2 A second article by Keynes (1921b), with the same title, appeared on 28 August. Wicksell's response, dated the day before, however, dealt only with the first one.

6 Emigration: a solution of the past

1 For an attempt to assess the effects of emigration from Sweden between 1860 and 1910 that builds on Wicksell's 1882 pamphlet, see Henriksson (1969).
2 On several occasions, Wicksell suggested that Sweden ought to join forces with Russia in military matters and perhaps even become part of the Russian empire (Gårdlund, 1996: 143–7, 182–3, 239–47). As Gårdlund (1990: 367–9) has pointed out, these suggestions were hardly taken seriously, but were seen mainly as provocations. However, in the light of his views of emigration, it cannot be discarded that they were more serious than what his contemporaries may have thought. (I am indebted to Bo Sandelin for pointing this out to me.)

3 O'Rourke and Williamson (1995: 173), in an article that highlights the importance of emigration and international trade as explanatory factors for the real-wage catch-up of Sweden on Britain and the United States between 1870 and 1913, argue that Wicksell 'asserted that emigration would solve the pauper problem that blighted labor-abundant and land-scarce Swedish agriculture' and refer to Wicksell's 'pro-emigration agitation.' The truth value of this statement depends on which of Wicksell's works on emigration you read. As the present chapter has demonstrated, the emigration issue was one (of the few) where Wicksell had problems arriving at a firm conviction.

7 The optimum population

1 In an article published both in English (Wicksell, 1910a; Overbeek, 1973) and German (Wicksell, 1910b) Wicksell uses the following formulation: '... what population size and density would ... guarantee everyone the maximum share of well-being and would thus, economically speaking, be the best' (Overbeek, 1973: 208).
2 For accounts of the Irish famine, see, for example, Woodham-Smith (1964) and Ó Gráda (1999).

9 Why was Wicksell accused of lack of originality?

1 Wicksell's stay in Cell No. 19 in Ystad was relatively comfortable (Gårdlund, 1996: 251–5; Andréasson, 1991: 90–1; Lundberg, 1991: 103, 107). He could work freely and his revision of the first chapter in his *Lectures*, on population, which was published as a separate booklet (Wicksell, 1979), was prefaced 'Ystad Jail, October 1909.'
2 The almost Byzantine manipulations to exclude Wicksell are well described in Gårdlund (1996: chapter 9). After the publication of *Über Wert, Kapital und Rente* in 1893, Wicksell had received a letter from Léon Walras, which concluded with the words that 'you have placed yourself among he first rank of the generation of mathematical economists that follows us (presumably meaning Walras himself) and which comprises Mr Irving Fisher of New Haven and Marquis Vilfredo Pareto, my successor at the University of Lausanne' (Hashimoto, forthcoming, Letter 18). International opinion, however, mattered little. Carl Uhr has argued that the Swedish academic spirit was parochial: '. . . parliament, in approving the position, had not voted enough money for a full professor's salary, so Wicksell had to accept it as professor *extraordinarius*, with the promise that the position would soon be upgraded' (Uhr, 1991a: 83). This was, however, delayed until January 1904. It was thus not until the age of fifty-three that Wicksell finally got the chair that he so well had deserved for a decade, but the reason was hardly the one given by Uhr. Rather, it was of a general, bureaucratic, kind. Until 1899, a professor who was *extraordinarius* could not become fully tenured because there would be no regular chair in his field. When this was changed, the reform was a half-hearted one, because professorships in different areas were linked to each other in a rotation system. When a fully tenured professor retired, a professor *extraordinarius* in a nearby subject would become fully tenured, while the successor to the one who had just retired would become *extraordinarius*. In the next round the opposite would apply, etc. It was mainly because of this that Wicksell at first became professor *extraordinarius* (Weibull, 1968: 249–53).

3   The Swedish original (Gårdlund, 1990: 242) has 'manic.'
4   This phrase has been omitted in the English translation of Gårdlund's book.
5   *Verdandi* was a radical student association founded in 1882, inspired to a large extent by Wicksell's views of social questions. Wicksell himself was one of the founders (Gårdlund, 1996: 72).
6   For reasons that are completely impossible to understand, the last chapter of Gårdlund's masterly biography of Wicksell, where a summary characteristic of Wicksell the person is offered, was never included in the English translation.
7   This – *To Educate the Swedish People* – was the title chosen by Lars and Christina Jonung for a recent book containing a number of Wicksell's unpublished writings (Jonung *et al.* 2001).
8   The translation into English comes from Swedberg (1999), p. 504.

References

[Åberg, Lawrence Heap; Davidson, David; Nilsson, A. and Bendixson, Artur] (1880), *Granskning av herr kand. K. Wicksells arbete om samhällsolyckornas vigtigaste orsak och botemedel*. Uppsala: Lundequistska Bokhandeln.

Åkerman, Johan (1933), 'Knut Wicksell, A Pioneer of Econometrics', *Econometrica*, Vol. 1.

Andréasson, Peter (1991), 'Hvita Briggen seglar vidare', *Ystadiana*, Vol. 19.

Becker, Gary S. (1975), 'A Theory of Marriage', in: Theodore W. Schultz (ed.), *Economics of the Family: Marriage, Children, and Human Capital*. Chicago: University of Chicago Press.

Blaug, Mark (1968), *Economic Theory in Retrospect*, 2nd edition. London: Heinemann.

Boianovsky, Mauro (2001), 'Economists as Demographers. Wicksell and Pareto on Population', in: Guido Erreygers (ed.), *Economics and Interdisciplinary Exchange*. London: Routledge.

Coleman, William (1985), 'Wicksell on Technical Change and Real Wages', *History of Political Economy*, Vol. 17.

Cornelius, Carl M. (1880), *Ett par ord i anledning af filosofie kandidaten Knut Wicksells framställning af "samhällsolyckornas vigtigaste orsak och botemedel"*. Uppsala: Akademiska Bokhandeln.

D'Avis, Eb. (1889), 'Die wirtschaftliche Ueberproduktion und die Mittel zu ihrer Abhilfe', *Jahrbücher für Nationalökonomie und Statistik*. N.F., Vol. 17.

Domar, Evsey D. (1970), 'The Causes of Slavery or Serfdom: A Hypothesis', *Journal of Economic History*, Vol. 30.

[Drysdale, George R.] as A doctor of medicine [pseud.] (1876), *The Elements of Social Science; or Physical, Sexual and Natural Religion. An Exposition of the True Cause and Only Cure of the Three Primary Social Evils: Poverty, Prostitution, and Celibacy*, 14th edition, enlarged. London: Edward Truelove.

—— as En medicine doktor [pseud.] (1878), *Samhällslärans grunddrag eller fysisk, sexuel och naturlig religion. En framställning af den verkliga orsaken till och af det enda botemedlet för samhällets tre förnämsta olyckor: fattigdom, prostitution och celibat*. Stockholm: Associations-Boktryckeriet.

Erlander, Tage (1972), *1901-1939*. Stockholm: Tidens Förlag.

Fahlbeck, Pontus (1902), 'Nymalthusianismen', *Statsvetenskaplig Tidskrift*, Vol. 4.

110   References

Findlay, Ronald (1993), 'International Trade and Factor Mobility with an Endogenous Land Frontier: Some General Equilibrium Consequences of Christopher Columbus', in: William Ethier, Elhanan Helpman and J. Peter Neary (eds), *Theory, Policy and Dynamics in International Trade.* Cambridge: Cambridge University Press.

—— (1995), *Factor Proportions, Trade, and Growth.* Cambridge, MA: MIT Press.

—— (1996), 'Towards a Model of Territorial Expansion and the Limits of Empire', in: Michelle F. Garfinkel and Stergios Skaperdas (eds), *The Political Economy of Conflict and Cooperation.* New York: Cambridge University Press.

Findlay, Ronald and Lundahl, Mats (1994), 'Natural Resources, 'Vent-for-Surplus', and the Staples Theory', in: Gerald M. Meier (ed.), *From Classical Economics to Development Economics.* New York: St. Martin's Press.

Fong, Monica S. (1976), 'Knut Wicksell's "The Two Population Problems"', *History of Political Economy*, Vol. 8.

Gårdlund, Torsten (1979), 'The Life of Knut Wicksell and Some Characteristics of His Works', in: Steinar Strøm and Björn Thalberg (eds), *The Theoretical Contributions of Knut Wicksell.* London: Macmillan.

—— (1990), *Knut Wicksell: Rebell i Det nya riket*, 2nd edition. Stockholm: SNS Förlag.

—— (1996), *The Life of Knut Wicksell.* Cheltenham, UK: Edward Elgar.

Goodwin, Richard (1979), 'Wicksell and the Malthusian Catastrophe', in: Steinar Strøm and Björn Thalberg (eds), *The Theoretical Contributions of Knut Wicksell.* London and Basingstoke: Macmillan.

Gottlieb, Manuel (1945), 'The Theory of Optimum Population for a Closed Economy', *Journal of Political Economy*, Vol. 53.

Gustafsson, Bo (1961), 'Svensk ekonomisk teori – Knut Wicksell 1851–1926', *Vår Tid*, Vol. 17.

Haberler, Gottfried (1936), *The Theory of International Trade.* Edinburgh: William Hodge.

Hamilton, Adolf Ludvig (1880), *Är öfverbefolkning i Sverige orsak till fattigdom; och är fattigdomen den vigtigaste orsaken till dryckenskap och otukt?* Uppsala: Uppsala Sedlighetsförening.

[Hammarskjöld, Carl Gustaf] as C.G.H. [pseud.] (1880), *Några ord med anledning af ett utkommet arbete omfattigdomens vigtigaste orsak och botemedel.* Stockholm: K. L. Beckman .

Hansson, Björn (1983), 'Wicksell's Critique of Ricardo's Chapter "On Machinery"', *Journal of Economic Studies*, Vol. 10.

Hashimoto, Hitoshi (1995), 'Biografiska och självbiografiska artiklar av Knut Wicksell samt 4 privatbrev', *KSU (Kyoto Sangyo University) Economic and Business Review*, No. 22.

—— (1996), 'Wicksells brev 1880–1885', *KSU (Kyoto Sangyo University) Economic and Business Review*, No. 23.

—— (1997), 'Wicksells brev 1886–1887', *KSU (Kyoto Sangyo University) Economic and Business Review*, No. 24.

—— (2001), 'Wicksell on Population'. Paper presented at The Wicksell Chair Centennial Symposium, 1–2 November, at Trolleholm Castle.

—— (forthcoming), *Selected Correspondence of Knut Wicksell: English, French and Italian Letters*. Manuscript, Kyoto Sangyo University.

Heckscher, Eli F. (1921), 'Knut Wicksell 70 år', *Dagens Nyheter*, 20 December.

—— (1991), 'The Effect of Foreign Trade on the Distribution of Income', in: Harry Flam and M. June Flanders (eds), *Heckscher-Ohlin Trade Theory*. Cambridge, MA: MIT Press.

Henriksson, Rolf G. H. (1969), '*An Interpretation of the Significance of Emigration for the Growth of Economic Welfare in Sweden, 1860–1910*', PhD dissertation, Department of Economics, Northwestern University, Evanston, IL.

—— (1991), 'The Facts on Wicksell on the Facts: Wicksell and Economic History', in: Joel Mokyr (ed.), The Vital One: Essays in Honour of Jonathan R.T. Hughes. *Research in Economic History*, Supplement No. 6.

Hofsten, Erland (1986), *Svensk befolkningshistoria: Några grunddrag i utvecklingen från 1750*. Stockholm: Rabén & Sjögren.

Hofsten, Erland and Lundström, Hans (1976), *Swedish Population History: Main Trends from 1750 to 1970*. Stockholm: National Central Bureau of Statistics.

Hutchinson, E.P. (1967), *The Population Debate. The Development of Conflicting Theories up to 1900*. Boston: Houghton Mifflin.

Jones, Ronald W. (1971), 'A Three-Factor Model in Theory, Trade, and History', in: Jagdish N. Bhagwati *et al.* (eds), *Trade, Balance of Payments and Growth: Papers in International Economics in Honor of Charles P. Kindleberger*. Amsterdam: North-Holland.

[Jönsson, Pelle] (arbetare i samhällslagrens djupa schakter) [pseud.] (1880), *Försök till en verklig kritik jämte några vidsträcktare synpunkter öfver kandidaten Knut Wicksells föredrag om samhällsolyckornas vigtigaste orsak och botemedel*. Stockholm: Aftonbladets Aktiebolags Tryckeri.

Jonung, Lars (1981), Introduction to Knut Wicksell, 'Ricardo on Machinery and the Present Unemployment', *Economic Journal*, Vol. 91.

—— (2001), 'Inledning', in: Lars Jonung, Torun Hedlund-Nyström and Christina Jonung (eds), *Att uppfostra det svenska folket. Knut Wicksells opublicerade manuskript*. Stockholm: SNS Förlag.

Jonung, Christina and Persson, Inga (1997), 'Anna and Knut', in: Inga Persson and Christina Jonung (eds), *Economics of the Family and Family Politics*. London: Routledge.

Jonung, Lars; Hedlund-Nyström, Torun and Jonung, Christina (eds) (2001), *Att uppfostra det svenska folket. Knut Wicksells opublicerade manuskript*. Stockholm: SNS Förlag.

Keynes, John Maynard (1919), *The Economic Consequences of the Peace*. London: Macmillan.

—— (1920), *Fredens ekonomiska följder*. Stockholm: Albert Bonniers Förlag.

—— (1921a), 'Ekonomiska framtidsperspektiv I. Den nya skadeståndsuppgörelsen', *Dagens Nyheter*, 18 August.

—— (1921b), 'Ekonomiska framtidperspektiv II. Skadeståndsuppgörelsen och världshandeln', *Dagens Nyheter*, 28 August.

—— (1929), 'The German Transfer Problem', *Economic Journal*, Vol. 39.

Knudtzon, Erik J. (1976), *Knut Wicksells tryckta skrifter 1868-1950*. Lund: CWK Gleerup.

Kock, Karin (1944), 'Nymalthusianismens genombrott i Sverige', in: *Studier i ekonomi och historia tillägnade Eli F. Heckscher på 65-årsdagen den 24 november 1944*. Uppsala: Almqvist & Wiksells Boktryckeri.

Kravis, Irving B. (1970), 'Trade as a Handmaiden of Growth: Similarities between the Nineteenth and Twentieth Centuries', *Economic Journal*, Vol. 80.

League of Nations (1945), *Industrialisation and Foreign Trade*. Geneva: League of Nations.

Leffler, Johan A. (1881), *Grundlinier till nationalekonomiken eller läran om folkens allmänna hushållning*. Stockholm: P.A. Nordstedt & Söner.

—— (1903), 'Robert Malthus, Professor P.E. Fahlbeck och Nymalthusianismen', *Ekonomisk Tidskrift*, Vol. 5.

Lewis, W. Arthur (1954), 'Economic Development with Unlimited Supplies of Labour', *Manchester School of Economic and Social Studies*, Vol. 22.

Lindahl, Erik (1958), 'Introduction: Wicksell's Life and Work', in: Knut Wicksell, *Selected Papers on Economic Theory*. London: George Allen & Unwin.

[Lindblom, Frans Petter], as –m [pseud.] (1880), *Några inlägg i Wicksellska frågan*. Uppsala: På författarens förlag.

Lundberg, Einar (1991), 'Berömdheter i cell 19', *Ystadiana*, Vol. 19.

Malthus, Thomas Robert (1989), *An Essay on the Principle of Population; Or A View of Its Past and Present Effects on Human Happiness; With an Inquiry into the Prospects Respecting the Future Removal or Mitigation of the Evils Which It Occasions* (ed. Patricia James). Two Volumes. Cambridge: Cambridge University Press.

Maneschi, Andrea (1998), *Comparative Advantage in International Trade: A Historical Perspective*. Cheltenham: Edward Elgar.

Mill, John Stuart (1929), *Principles of Political Economy* (ed. W.J. Ashley), new edition. London: Longmans, Green and Co.

Mundell, Robert A. (2002), 'Keynes and Ohlin on the Transfer Problem', in: Ronald Findlay, Lars Jonung and Mats Lundahl (eds), *Bertil Ohlin: A Centennial Celebration (1899–1999)*. Cambridge, MA: MIT Press.

Myrdal, Gunnar (1972), *Vetenskap och politik i nationalekonomin*, new revised edition. Stockholm: Rabén & Sjögren.

Myrdal, Alva and Myrdal, Gunnar (1935), *Kris i befolkningsfrågan*, 3rd edition. Stockholm: Albert Bonniers Förlag.

Nordin, Svante (1981), *Den Boströmska skolan och den svenska idealismens fall*. Lund: Doxa.

Nordqvist, Liv Wicksell (1985), *Anna Bugge Wicksell: En kvinna före sin tid*. Malmö: Liber Förlag.

Ó Gráda, Cormac (1999), *Black '47 and Beyond: The Great Irish Famine in History, Economy, and Memory*. Princeton, NJ: Princeton University Press.

Ohlin, Bertil (1929), 'The Reparation Problem: A Discussion', *Economic Journal*, Vol. 39.

—— (1933), *Interregional and International Trade*. Cambridge, MA: Harvard University Press.

—— (1991), 'The Theory of Trade', in: Harry Flam and M. June Flanders (eds), *Heckscher-Ohlin Trade Theory*. Cambridge, MA: MIT Press .

[Öhrvall, Hjalmar], as En läkare [pseud.] (1886), *Försigtighetsmått i ägtenskapet. En framställning af de s k preventiva medlen af en läkare*. Stockholm: Kungsholms Bokhandel.

O'Rourke, Kevin Hjortshøj and Williamson, Jeffrey G. (1995), 'Open Economy Forces and Late Nineteenth Century Swedish Catch-Up. A Quantitative Accounting', *Scandinavian Economic History Review*, Vol. 43.

Overbeek, Johannes (1973), 'Wicksell on Population', *Economic Development and Cultural Change*, Vol. 21.

Pålsson Syll, Lars (2002), *De ekonomiska teoriernas historia*, third edition. Lund: Studentlitteratur.

Pitchford, J.D. (1974), *Population in Economic Growth*. Amsterdam: North-Holland.

Ribbing, Seved (1889), *Om den sexuela hygienen och några af dess etiska konsekvenser. Trenne föredrag*. Stockholm: Wilhelm Bille.

Ricardo, David (1971), *On the Principles of Political Economy and Taxation*, 3rd edition. Harmondsworth: Penguin Books.

Robbins, Lionel (1927), 'The Optimum Theory of Population', in: *London Essays in Economics: In Honor of Edwin Cannan* (eds T. E. Gregory and Hugh Dalton). London: Routledge.

Robertson, Dennis H. (1938), 'The Future of International Trade', *Economic Journal*, Vol. 48.

Rohtlieb, Curt (1916), 'Om gränsen för jordbrukets intensifiering', *Ekonomisk Tidskrift*, Vol. 18.

Samuelson, Paul A. (1939), 'The Gains from International Trade', *Canadian Journal of Economics and Political Science*, Vol. 5.

—— (1948), 'International Trade and Equalisation of Factor Prices', *Economic Journal*, Vol. 58.

—— (1949), 'International Factor-Price Equalisation Once Again', *Economic Journal*, Vol. 59.

—— (1953), 'Prices of Factors and Goods in General Equilibrium', *Review of Economic Studies*, Vol. 21.

—— (1971a), 'An Exact Hume-Ricardo-Marshall Model of International Trade', *Journal of International Economics*, Vol. 1.

—— (1971b), 'Ohlin Was Right', *Swedish Journal of Economics*, Vol. 73.

—— (1989), 'Ricardo Was Right', *Scandinavian Journal of Economics*, Vol. 91.

Schumpeter, Joseph A. (1954), *History of Economic Analysis*. New York: Oxford University Press.

Shackle, G. L. S. (1954), 'Foreword to the English Translation' in: Knut Wicksell, *Value, Capital and Rent*. London: George Allen & Unwin.

Skidelsky, Robert (1992), *John Maynard Keynes: The Economist as Saviour 1920-1937*. London: Macmillan.

Sommarin, Emil (1926–27), 'Minnesord över professor Knut Wicksell', i: Kungliga Humanistiska Vetenskapssamfundet i Lund, *Årsberättelse1926/27*. Lund.

114   References

—— (1947), *Studenter och arbetare. Minnen av skånsk arbetarrörelse och lundensisk radikalism*. Lund: C.W.K Gleerups Förlag.

Spengler, Joseph (1983), 'Knut Wicksell, Father of the Optimum', *Atlantic Economic Journal*, Vol. 11.

Stolper, Wolfgang F. and Samuelson, Paul A. (1941), 'Protection and Real Wages', *Review of Economic Studies*, Vol. 9.

Swedberg, Richard (1998), 'Knut Wicksell – en samhällsvetenskaplig klassiker', in: Richard Swedberg (ed.), Knut Wicksell, *Stridsskrifter och samhällsekonomiska analyser*. Stockholm: City University Press.

—— (1999), 'Civil Courage (*Zivilcourage*): The Case of Knut Wicksell', *Theory and Society*, Vol. 28.

Uhr, Carl G. (1951), 'Knut Wicksell – A Centennial Evaluation', *American Economic Review*, Vol. 41.

—— (1962), *Economic Doctrines of Knut Wicksell*. Berkeley: University of California Press.

—— (1975), *Economic Doctrines of David Davidson*. Uppsala: Almqvist & Wiksell International.

—— (1991a), 'Knut Wicksell, Neoclassicist and Iconoclast', in: Bo Sandelin (ed.), *The History of Swedish Economic Thought*. London: Routledge.

—— (1991b), 'David Davidson: The Transition to Neoclassical Economics', in: Bo Sandelin (ed.), *The History of Swedish Economic Thought*. London: Routledge.

Weibull, Jörgen (1968), *Lunds universitets historia, IV. 1868–1968*. Lund: CWK Gleerup.

Wicksell, Knut (1880a), *Några ord om samhällsolyckornas vigtigaste orsak och botemedel med särskild afseende på dryckenskapen*. Uppsala: På författarens förlag.

—— (1880b), *Svar till mina granskare. Med ett tillägg: Om ny-malthusianismens nuvarande ställning och utsigter i Europa*. Uppsala: Esaias Edquists Boktryckeri.

—— (1882), *Om utvandringen. Dess betydelse och orsaker*. Stockholm: Albert Bonniers Förlag.

—— (1887a), *Om folkökningen i Sverge och de faror den medför för det allmänna välståndet och för sedligheten*. Stockholm: Kungsholms Bokhandel.

—— (1887b), *Om prostitutionen. Huru mildra och motverka detta samhällsonda? Två föredrag*. Stockholm: Kungsholms Bokhandel.

—— (1890a), *De sexuela frågorna. Granskning av hrr Emil Svenséns, Björnstjerne Björnsons samt professor Seved Ribbings broschyrer*. Stockholm: Kungsholms Bokhandel.

—— (1890b), 'En sjelfbiografi, med porträtt', *Fritänkaren, Organ för Sveriges Utilister*, No. 22, 15 November 1890.

—— (1890c), 'Tomme maver – og fulde magasiner', *Samtiden*, Vol. 1.

—— (1891), *La population, les causes de ses progrès et les obstacles qui en arrêtent l'essor*. Pièce destinée ou concours Rossi, 1891. Manuscript. Paris: Académie des sciences morales et politiques de l'Institut de France.

—— (1892), 'Normalarbetsdag', dated 1892, in: Lars Jonung, Torun Hedlund-Nyström and Christina Jonung (eds) (2001), *Att uppfostra det svenska folket. Knut Wicksells opublicerade manuskript*. Stockholm: SNS Förlag.

—— (1896), *Finanzteoretische Untersuchungen nebst Darstellung und Kritik des Steuerwesens Schwedens*. Jena: Verlag von Gustav Fischer.

—— (1901), *Föreläsningar i nationalekonomi. Första delen: Teoretisk nationalekonomi*. Lund: Berlingska Boktryckeriet.

—— (1902), 'Professor Fahlbeck om nymalthusianismen', *Ekonomisk Tidskrift*, Vol. 4.

—— (1903), 'Om begreppen produktivitet, rentabilitet och relativ avkastning inom jordbruket', *Ekonomisk Tidskrift*, Vol. 5.

—— (1909), *Tronen, altaret, svärdet och pänningpåsen. Föredrag hållet i Folkets Hus den 2 november 1908*. Stockholm: Östermalmstryckeriet.

—— (1910a), 'The Optimum of Population', *The Malthusian*, Vol. 34.

—— (1910b), 'Das Optimum der Bevölkerung', *Die neue Generation*, Vol. 6.

—— (1911), 'Insändare till Aftontidningen', dated 24 December, in: Lars Jonung, Torun Hedlund-Nyström and Christina Jonung (eds) (2001), *Att uppfostra det svenska folket. Knut Wicksells opublicerade manuskript*. Stockholm: SNS Förlag.

—— (1914), *'Allvarliga farhågor'*. Stockholm: Sällskapet för Humanitär Barnalstring.

—— (1916a), 'Fosterfördrivning, religion och moral', dated fall, in: Lars Jonung, Torun Hedlund-Nyström and Christina Jonung (eds) (2001), *Att uppfostra det svenska folket. Knut Wicksells opublicerade manuskript*. Stockholm: SNS Förlag.

—— (1916b), 'La guerre, la paix et l'acroissement de la population', *Scientia*, Vol. 10.

—— (1921a), 'Det tyska skadeståndet', dated May, in: Lars Jonung, Torun Hedlund-Nyström and Christina Jonung (eds) (2001), *Att uppfostra det svenska folket. Knut Wicksells opublicerade manuskript*. Stockholm: SNS Förlag.

—— (1921b), 'Det tyska skadeståndet', *Dagens Nyheter*, 27 August.

—— (1921c), 'Kristen etik och personlig profylax', dated March, in: Lars Jonung, Torun Hedlund-Nyström and Christina Jonung (eds) (2001), *Att uppfostra det svenska folket. Knut Wicksells opublicerade manuskript*. Stockholm: SNS Förlag.

—— (1922), 'Tyska skadeståndet – en befolkningsfråga', dated end of 1922, in: Lars Jonung, Torun Hedlund-Nyström and Christina Jonung (eds) (2001), *Att uppfostra det svenska folket. Knut Wicksells opublicerade manuskript*. Stockholm: SNS Förlag.

—— (1923), 'Tysklands betalningskraft', dated 1923, in: Lars Jonung, Torun Hedlund-Nyström and Christina Jonung (eds) (2001), *Att uppfostra det svenska folket. Knut Wicksells opublicerade manuskript*. Stockholm: SNS Förlag.

—— (1924/25), 'Befolkningsfrågan och sunda förnuftet', undated, in: Lars Jonung, Torun Hedlund-Nyström and Christina Jonung (eds) (2001), *Att uppfostra det svenska folket. Knut Wicksells opublicerade manuskript*. Stockholm: SNS Förlag.

—— (1925), *Barnalstringsfrågan: Föredrag, hållet vid Nymalthusianska sällskapet*. Stockholm: Federativs Förlag.

—— (1926a), *Läran om befolkningen, dess sammansättning och förändringar*. 2nd edition. Med ledning av författarens efterlämnade anteckningar. Utgiven av Sven Wicksell. Stockholm: Studentföreningen Verdandis småskrifter.

—— (1926b), 'Befolkningsfrågan och världsfreden', dated 12 January, in: Lars Jonung, Torun Hedlund-Nyström and Christina Jonung (eds) (2001), *Att uppfostra det svenska folket. Knut Wicksells opublicerade manuskript*. Stockholm: SNS Förlag.

—— (1934), *Lectures on Political Economy*. Vol. One: *General Theory*. London: George Routledge and Sons.

—— (1954), *Value, Capital and Rent*. London: George Allen & Unwin.

—— (1958a), 'The "Critical Point" in the Law of Decreasing Agricultural Productivity', in: *Selected Papers on Economic Theory*. London: George Allen & Unwin.

—— (1958b), 'Marginal Productivity as the Basis of Distribution in Economics', in: *Selected Papers on Economic Theory*. London: George Allen & Unwin.

—— (1978), 'The World War: An Economist's View', *Scandinavian Journal of Economics*, Vol. 80.

—— (1979), 'The Theory of Population, Its Composition and Changes', in: Steinar Strøm and Björn Thalberg (eds), *The Theoretical Contributions of Knut Wicksell*. London and Basingstoke: Macmillan .

—— (1981), 'Ricardo on Machinery and the Present Unemployment: An Unpublished Manuscript by Knut Wicksell', *Economic Journal*, Vol. 91.

—— (1999a), 'A Few Remarks on the Chief Cause of Social Misfortunes and the Best Means to Remedy Them, With Particular Reference to Drunkenness', in: Bo Sandelin (ed.), Knut Wicksell, *Selected Essays in Economics*, Vol. II. London: Routledge.

—— (1999b), 'Can a Country Become Underpopulated?', in: Bo Sandelin (ed.), Knut Wicksell, *Selected Essays in Economics, Volume II*. London and New York: Routledge.

—— (1999c), 'Overproduction – or Overpopulation?', in: Bo Sandelin (ed.), Knut Wicksell, *Selected Essays in Economics,* Vol. II. London and New York: Routledge.

—— (1999d), 'From *The Emigration Inquiry*, Appendix 18', in: Bo Sandelin (ed.), Knut Wicksell, *Selected Essays in Economics, Volume II*. London: Routledge.

Wigforss, Ernst (1950), *Minnen. I. Före 1914*. Stockholm: Tidens Förla.

Woodham-Smith, Cecil (1964), *The Great Hunger: Ireland 1845–9*. London: Readers Union, Hamish Hamilton.

Index